PALESTINIAN RESISTANCE LITERATURE UNDER OCCUPATION, 1948–1968

PALESTINIAN RESISTANCE LITERATURE UNDER OCCUPATION, 1948–1968

Ghassan Kanafani

Translated by
Tarif Khalidi

VERSO
London • New York

مؤسسة الدراسات الفلسطينية
Institute for Palestine Studies

Published in collaboration with the Institute for Palestine Studies
English-language edition first published by Verso 2026
First published in Arabic as *Al-Adab Al-Filistīni Al-Muqāwim Taḥt Al-Iḥtilāl: 1948-1968* by the Institute for Palestine Studies in 1968

The manufacturer's authorized representative in the EU for product safety (GPSR) is LOGOS EUROPE, 9 rue Nicolas Poussin, 17000, La Rochelle, France
Contact@logoseurope.eu

1 3 5 7 9 10 8 6 4 2

Verso
UK: 6 Meard Street, London W1F 0EG
US: 207 East 32nd Street, New York, NY 10016
versobooks.com

Verso is the imprint of New Left Books

ISBN-13: 978-1-8367-4445-0

British Library Cataloguing in Publication Data
A catalogue record for this book is available from the British Library

Library of Congress Cataloging-in-Publication Data

Names: Kanafānī, Ghassān author | Khalidi, Tarif, 1938- translator
Title: Palestinian resistance literature under occupation, 1948-1968 / Ghassan Kanafani; translated by Tarif Khalidi.
Other titles: Adab al-Filasṭīnī al-muqāwim taḥtha al-iḥtilāl, 1948-1968. English
Description: English-language edition. | London; New York: Verso, 2026. | Includes bibliographical references.
Identifiers: LCCN 2026004872 | ISBN 9781836744450 trade paperback
Subjects: LCSH: Arabic literature--Palestine--History and criticism | LCGFT: Literary criticism
Classification: LCC PJ8190.I8 K2813 2026
LC record available at https://lccn.loc.gov/2026004872

Typeset in Garamond by Biblichor Ltd, Scotland
Printed and bound by CPI Group (UK) Ltd, Croydon CR0 4YY

To my father
and to the spirit of my mother
the wings of resistance that carried me
past the hardship of defeats and bitterness

Contents

Foreword

Ghassan Kanafani's writing was considered so dangerous to the Zionist enterprise that Israeli agents assassinated him in 1972 with a car bomb, along with his seventeen-year-old niece, Lamis. Kanafani was thirty-six years old at the time. Having met him and having been deeply impressed by his personality and his intelligence, I was among the tens of thousands of mourners who walked behind his coffin. A prolific and gifted writer of fiction and plays, he was a dedicated revolutionary, a militant editorialist and journalist, a talented graphic artist, and one of the most perceptive chroniclers of the history of Palestinian resistance in its many forms. *Palestinian Resistance Literature Under Occupation, 1948–1968*, here translated into English by Tarif Khalidi for the first time since its original publication in Arabic in 1968, reveals Kanafani to also have been an able literary critic and an insightful analyst of Palestinian society inside Israel in the two decades after the Nakba of 1948. Like all his work, this book resonates with Kanafani's burning commitment to the Palestinian cause.

Kanafani's reputation among readers, academics, activists, and militants has only continued to grow in the decades since his murder. His work, especially his novels, novellas, and short stories, are widely published and read in Arabic, English, and other languages, and are taught in Arabic literature courses all over the world. It is harder to access some of the rest of Kanafani's wide-ranging written output, especially his extensive political and journalistic writings. These are mainly found in Beirut newspapers and periodicals of the 1960s and early '70s, notably in the journal of the Popular Front for the Liberation of Palestine, *al-Hadaf*, which he founded and edited until his assassination.

However, a few of Kanafani's political writings have been translated into English, as has his far-ranging dissection of Zionist literature. Perhaps the most important of these translated works is his seminal essay on the great Palestinian revolt of the late 1930s. This nuanced class analysis remains the best account to date of the causes for the revolt and the reasons for its failure, and for its continuing resonance among Palestinians to this day.[1] This work has informed the interpretations of historians and other writers who followed Kanafani in assessing the impact of the revolt and its aftermath.

Kanafani's writing, especially his fiction, is popular in much of the world, and specialists in modern Arabic literature place

1 Ghassan Kanafani, *The Revolution of 1936–1939 in Palestine: Background, Details and Analysis*, trans. Hazem Jamjoum, with an introduction by Layan Fuleihan and an afterword by Maher Charif, New York: 1804 Books, 2023. Also recently translated are Ghassan Kanafani, *Ghassan Kanafani: Selected Political Writings*, eds. Louis Brehony and Tahrir Hamdi, London: Pluto Press, 2024, and *On Zionist Literature*, trans. Mahmoud Najib, with a preface by Anni Kanafani and an introduction by Steven Salaita, London: Ebb Press, 2022.

him in the first rank of Palestinian writers. However, his work has met with sustained, bitter resistance from those who oppose any form of advocacy for Palestinian liberation. As only one example, an adaptation for the stage of one of Kanafani's best-known novels, *Men in the Sun*, which was to have been performed in Nazareth in October 1977, was banned by the Israeli authorities. Similarly, a theatrical adaptation in English of Kanafani's novella *Returning to Haifa* was commissioned by the Public Theater in New York about a decade ago, but was never staged because of the last-minute opposition of the theater's board, on the supposed grounds that Kanafani was a "terrorist." This extraordinary work has as one of its protagonists a Jewish Israeli Holocaust survivor, who is sensitively portrayed by Kanafani. Thus, having assassinated him, his enemies continue to pursue Kanafani in death decades later. The theatrical adaptation of this work nevertheless premiered at the Finborough Theater in London in February 2018 to excellent reviews, has been published,[2] and has been translated into several languages.[3]

One of the most striking things about Kanafani's lengthy opening essay on the resistance literature he selected for this volume is his constant stress on the importance of language, words, and culture in the arsenal of resistance. He writes, "The poetry of resistance . . . does not begin by demeaning the value of words in that bitter struggle. Rather, it is fully cognizant of

2 Adapted by Ismail Khalidi and Naomi Wallace, the play was published as *Returning to Haifa*, London: Faber & Faber, 2018.

3 The play has been translated into French and received a staged reading. *Returning to Haifa* has also been translated, dramatized and adapted for the stage in several other languages and countries. It has been very well received by the public and received good reviews in the press.

the role of words, which it sanctifies . . ." Speaking of "resistance in the widest sense of the term," he adds: "This type of resistance assumes its most original form in political and cultural action . . . It follows that the cultural dimension of resistance is of the utmost importance and is no less valuable than armed resistance." Kanafani himself obviously practiced what he preached, skillfully wielding words as his weapon in the Palestinian liberation struggle.

This sophisticated understanding of the many dimensions of resistance, and of the value of culture in the struggle for liberation, is only one reason why Kanafani's writing is so rich in lessons for those seeking guidance in resisting oppression, and why it offers such valuable advice for activists and militants. That understanding is certainly shared by Israel's security establishment, as is evidenced by its assassinations of a multiplicity of Palestinian intellectuals, artists, and writers, ranging from Ghassan Kanafani, Kamal Nasser, and Wael Zwaiter to the more recent murders of Refaat Alareer, Hiba Abu Nada, Inas al-Saqa, and numerous other writers, artists, journalists, and cultural figures during Israel's genocidal war on Gaza.

As notable as Kanafani's nuanced treatment of literature and culture as central elements of resistance is his exposition of the situation of Palestinians living under Israeli rule from 1948 until 1968. Writing from Beirut and thus deprived of direct contact with those inside the parts of Palestine occupied in 1948, Kanafani nevertheless offers a striking and detailed portrait of the subtle and overt forms of repression to which this segment of Palestinian society was subjected. His description of the ways in which Palestinian writers, teachers, and thinkers in Israel were constantly harassed, placed under house arrest, and imprisoned is particularly forceful. Kanafani shows that far from enjoying equal rights with Jewish Israelis, second-class Palestinian citizens were subject to nearly two decades of martial law, movement restrictions, constant spying, and frequently overt pressure from the General Security Services, or Shin Bet, as well as Israel's military intelligence services. This repression was in service of the Israeli regime's effort to colonize not only the lands but also the minds of the Palestinians under its control.

Although writing from a distance, Kanafani was clearly able to closely follow the details of Israel's persecution of Mahmoud Darwish, Samih al-Qasim, and many other notable writers who feature in this book. Combined with his description of the social and economic situation of Palestinian communities in the areas of Palestine seized by Israel in 1948, Kanafani offered readers in 1968 one of the earliest portraits available of that part of Palestinian society, cut off as it was from the rest of the Palestinian people. In so doing, he was helping to counter a false impression of those Palestinians who managed to remain there after Israel's occupation as somehow "traitors" to the Arab cause. By not only portraying the unending repression to which they were subjected but also highlighting the centrality of resistance to their writings, Kanafani was showing his readers outside Palestine that these Palestinians remained linked to the rest of their people, and indeed in many cases were exemplars of resistance to Zionist oppression.

Yet another connective feature of this work is Kanafani's highlighting of the Arab nationalist sentiments expressed by the literature that he focuses on in this book. He thereby both shows that these writers were responding to the same influences as Arab writers elsewhere and reinforces his argument that Palestinians living under Israeli control were an integral part of their people. Far from seeing these and other Arab nationalist aspects of their work as derivative, Kanafani indeed describes it as on occasion superior to the literature produced in other parts of the Arab world.

Finally, although Kanafani himself says that "the present study [is] more in the nature of a documentary study, as it were, than a literary analysis," declining to lay claim to any literary merit for his work, it in fact constitutes a substantial contribution to Palestinian literature and indeed to Palestinian literary criticism. The selections made by Kanafani in 1968 have more than withstood the test of time in terms of literary merit: Mahmoud Darwish, Samih al-Qasim, Tawfiq Zayyad, Fawzi al-Asmar, Rashid Hussein, Tawfiq Fayyad, and "Abu Salam" (the nom de plume of Emile Habibi), among others he cited or whose work he selected, today stand even higher in the pantheon of Palestinian and Arab literature than they did in his day. Indeed, Kanafani was one of the first, if not the first, to discover the merits of poets like Mahmoud Darwish and Samih al-Qasim who are revered today. If there is any absence in this collection, it may be the lack of a mention of a single female author. This absence can be attributed to the entrenched patriarchal nature of Palestinian society, as well as the deprivation to which Palestinians inside Israel were subjected by Israeli military rule in those early years of its occupation, conditions to which Kanafani makes reference several times.

Because of these and its many other merits, the Institute for Palestine Studies, together with Verso Books, and with the gracious support of the Ghassan Kanafani Cultural Foundation and the estate of Ghassan Kanafani, take pleasure in presenting to English readers for the first time this translation of one of Ghassan Kanafani's most important works.

Rashid Khalidi
New York, December 1, 2025

Introduction

Armed resistance is not merely skin-deep; it is the fruit of a tree with roots firmly planted in the ground. Though liberation may emerge from the muzzle of a rifle, the rifle itself is rooted in the will to be liberated, which, in turn, is nothing but the natural, logical, and inevitable result of resistance in the widest sense of the term: resistance as rejection and as firm adherence to roots and principles.

This type of resistance assumes its most original form in political and cultural action, and these two concomitant and complementary actions are in turn the fertile soil that breeds armed resistance, nurtures it, ensures its continuity, and surrounds it with safeguards.

It follows that the cultural dimension of resistance is of the utmost importance and is no less valuable than armed resistance. Therefore, it is urgently necessary to observe that dimension in detail, and to explore it, if we are to understand the ground in which the weapons of armed resistance are planted.

Arab intellectuals in occupied Palestine in the period between 1948 and 1968, living under the cruelest circumstances of repression and cultural confinement, present us with a historic example of the literature of resistance, with all its conscious awareness and unwavering vigor and, more importantly, its persistence, reach, and depth.

In fact, the literature of resistance was never an emergent phenomenon in Palestinian cultural life. In this respect, and in terms of both cultural and armed resistance, the Palestinian resistance movement provides us with early and fundamental examples to guide the contemporary pan-Arab path of struggle.

Since the decade of the 1930s, at least, Palestinian history has displayed numerous instances of both armed and cultural resistance. Just as armed revolts by the people of Palestine produced figures such as `Izz al-Din al-Qassam, the literature of resistance also produced, before and after him, figures of the same standing whom the Arab world still remembers with a great deal of pride, most prominently Ibrahim Tuqan, `Abd al-Rahim Mahmud, "Abu Salma" (`Abd al-Karim al-Karmi), and others.

When seen in this light, the current Palestinian literature of resistance, just like armed resistance, constitutes a new link in a historic chain that has never been severed from the life of the Palestinian people in the last half century. However, what distinguishes the resistance literature produced from 1948 to 1968 is the exceptionally cruel and violent circumstances that its authors experienced and challenged. One might say it was the oven in which that people produced the "bread" of its cultural productions, on a daily basis.

Obtaining examples of that literature was a task fraught with difficulties. It is now evident that there are exemplars that were never published, and we still do not know if they can be published in the near future. Likewise, we were unable to access a sizable heritage of Palestinian popular poetry, born, bred, and widely spread in rural Palestine over the last twenty years or so, and thus could not use it in a separate study, though there are some ongoing and promising efforts being exerted to do so today.

It must also be pointed out that this present study is not a new or revised edition of an earlier book of mine, entitled *The Literature of Resistance in Occupied Palestine*, published by Dar al-Adab. Instead, it ought to be regarded as being, to a large extent, complementary to that earlier volume, a further step in its direction. I must therefore point out that the earlier volume constitutes a necessary introduction to the present work whether in its analysis or in the examples cited.

To expand this formal but important point, two observations must be made:

First, we made sure that most of the examples selected for this anthology are neither found in current anthologies nor soon to be published in separate poetry collections.

Second, numerous analytic studies of the literature of resistance are currently being undertaken by scholars expert in literary criticism and research, making the present study more in the nature of a documentary study, as it were, than a literary analysis.

Finally, this study is chiefly concerned with the attempt to provide another documentary record of the Palestinian literature of resistance three years after the earlier volume mentioned above. If it succeeds in doing so, it has no other ambition.

Beirut, April 15, 1968
Ghassan Kanafani

I

The Cultural Environment of the Arabs in Occupied Palestine

An Arab writer in occupied Palestine, Fawzi al-Asmar, tells the following story: "While having lunch in a Tel Aviv restaurant I overheard the following phone conversation. The speaker was a young man from one of the villages of the Triangle (*Muthallath*) which I later learned was Umm al-Fahm:

"'Hello, Vaed Hapoel?[1] Could you please pass me on to Mr. Qassab in the Arab Department?' (The whole conversation was in Hebrew.) 'Hello, Mr. Qassab? Greetings. Ahmad speaking. Did you receive my letter? I am very sorry I wrote it in Hebrew and asked my friend Qasim to translate it into Arabic. I'm sorry. I just finished Hebrew secondary school and I don't know how to write in Arabic, so I asked him to translate it.'"

1 Hebrew for "Workers' Committee."

Al-Asmar continues:

"A passing conversation, but of great import. Here I don't solely blame Ahmad for not knowing how to write in Arabic, his mother tongue, but I do blame Ahmad in part. Is he not ashamed of himself? I do not deny the fact that the authorities are trying to confuse the minds of the young generation of Arabs. But what about his own responsibility? I address myself here to that Ahmad and to every other Ahmad and say to them: 'Go quickly and learn your mother tongue or else . . .'"[2]

This brief but deeply wounding vignette sheds light upon a unique kind of cultural struggle undertaken by the Arabs under occupation[3] since 1948 to defend their language, culture, and heritage. In fact, this battle represents one of the ugliest means employed by a settler colonialist regime to obliterate a national movement and uproot it totally. For us to recognize fully the value of the literature of resistance in occupied Palestine, by way of what it has produced in the last

2 Fawzi al-Asmar, in *Haolam Hazeh* (*This World*), a weekly magazine published in Hebrew, no. 39 (June 1967).

3 It is useful to cite here a number of very significant statistics regarding the Arabs under occupation that could constitute the necessary background for future research and help in understanding it. These statistics are taken from a book entitled *Israel Today*, published by the Histadrut Organization and edited by Yehuda Gotthelf in 1967. He in turn derived these figures from *Hamizrah Hehadash* (*The New East*), p. 23, which states: "Around 300,000 Arabs live in the occupied territories (about 11% of the population), 69% of whom are Muslim, 22% Christian, and 9% Druze. The birth rate among Arabs is very high. According to 1963 figures, half the Arab population was less than 15 years old, 75% was less than 30 years old, and 20% was less than 4 years old. Three quarters of the Arabs in Israel live in villages and there are six villages with populations in excess of five thousand. There are 27,000 Arabs who live in Nazareth, 8,000 in Shafa `Amr, 5,900 in Tel-Aviv and Jaffa, 10,700 in Haifa, 7,250 in Acre, 2,500 in Ramla, and 1,850 in Lydda. Some 60,000 Arab men and 9,000 Arab women constitute a manual labor force in Israeli towns, and half of all Arab wage workers work outside their place of residence."

twenty years, we need to be aware of the immensity of the daily obstacles that pose challenges to Arabic cultural life under occupation.

Here, then, is an astonishing and explicit statement in this connection, made by an Israeli intellectual during an open and recorded interview. This man says: "I believe that our national existence supersedes all other considerations including ethical considerations. The presence of an Arab minority in Israel represents the greatest danger to Israel, if not now or in the near future, then in the long term. To avert that danger, we must do everything possible in a manner that does not provoke international condemnation. We need to use a suitable cover and attractive language. However, if absolutely necessary, we should ignore international public opinion.

"We should limit their progress and seize their lands. Every Arab who finishes secondary school or university should not be employed by us. Let him look for a job for three, four, or five years until he despairs and understands that there is no place for him in this country. Let him seek employment in some other country. We must convince the Arabs not to listen to Arab radio stations. We must isolate them from Arabic culture and subject them to the influence of Jewish culture.

"Q. What happens if they decide to continue to listen to Egyptian Radio? And if they do not understand that hint and leave the country, what then?

"A. They will understand, and they will emigrate.

"Q. What if they refuse to abandon their cultural and national identity or refuse to emigrate?

"A. No, they will understand!

"Q. Be frank and say it outright: We will need to build an Auschwitz!"[4]

This exchange is not in the realm of theoretical fantasy; it is an expression of a daily and experienced reality. It is now a well-known fact that "the educational standard in Arab schools is far inferior to that in Jewish schools, in addition to the fact that qualified Arab teachers are routinely dismissed and replaced by others who have only completed their elementary education."[5]

A policy of deliberate stultification is a prominent aspect of Zionist cultural repression of the Arabs under occupation. It is in this context that the question of education and its low standards in the Arab sphere has become a central issue.

In an article published in a book entitled *Israel Today*, Z. Aran admits[6] that "53% of all Arab teachers in Israel are unqualified." In the same book, M. Asaf states:[7] "The lack of teachers, books, and planning in Arab secondary schools in Israel has led to considerable levels of failure in the secondary school (matriculation) exams," adding that Jewish society "has been unable to absorb either Arab graduates of secondary schools or Arab university graduates," and that "there is an even larger problem for Arabs who are forced to abandon their secondary education."

Asaf grants that the percentage of Arab graduates from Israeli universities is low but cites no figures. Despite this, we

---

4 *Haolam Hazeh*, no. 38 (May 1967). Auschwitz was a Nazi concentration camp in Poland, which witnessed mass extermination of Jews in gas chambers.

5 Shalom Cohen, ibid.

6 Gotthelf (ed.), *Israel Today*, p. 121.

7 Ibid., p. 47.

can imagine what that percentage might be when that same writer makes a further and more alarming admission by stating that in 1967 the total number of Arab students in Israeli universities was 200, compared with 19,000 Israelis.

Moreover, we have yet another alarming statistic: "Of the generation of Arabs who began first grade in 1957, 45% had left school by 1964, i.e., before they reached grade 8."[8]

If this is the situation in elementary education, it must be even bleaker in secondary and university education. Asaf states that only 10 percent of Arabs who sat for the secondary school certificate in 1964 passed, while the passing rate in 1963 was 12 percent.[9]

This figure is clearly deceptive, since other sources state that the pass rate was never more than 4 or 5 percent, whereas Z. Aran affirms that the pass rate in secondary school exams among the Arabs of Israel in 1963 was 40.2 percent.[10] What underlines the seriousness of this issue is the two widely divergent figures cited by Asaf and Aran of Arab secondary school pass rates for the same year and in the same book!

In addition to all this, we possess a brief but definitive description of the educational system among the Arabs of occupied Palestine that gives an almost complete idea of the true reality. In a memorandum submitted to United Nations Secretary General U Thant in early 1964, the Al-Ard Association in Israel stated:[11]

---

8 Ahmad al-Khatib, *Al-Ittihad* (Arabic language newspaper published by the Communist Party in Israel), Tel Aviv, March 29, 1968.

9 Gotthelf (ed.), *Israel Today*, p. 47.

10 Ibid., p. 121.

11 The full text of the memorandum was published in the "Palestine Supplement" of the Beirut newspaper *Al-Muharrir* in its issue of January 14, 1965. *The*

"The high levels of education under the British Mandate have plummeted in the past sixteen years. The pass rate in the matriculation certificate (Bagrut) in Arab schools under the direct supervision of the Israeli Ministry of Education is a mere 4 or 5%.

"This precipitous decline is due to the following reasons:

"1. Interference in educational matters, which is both harmful and outrageous, by officials of the military administration and intelligence services (Shin Bet). These two services have the last word in the choice of teachers, without the least regard to their professional qualifications. Teachers are chosen on the basis of the services they provide to the military and intelligence agencies and are expected to be compliant, colluding with the occupation and disseminating propaganda for the ruling party.

"2. The lack of sufficient schools. Despite the constant increase in student numbers, the number of schools is still very limited, and the Ministry of Education deliberately ignores the law of compulsory education as it applies to the Arab minority.

"3. A severe shortage of textbooks, labs, educational equipment, maps, and libraries.

"4. Some responsible officials misuse their office to publish low-quality textbooks, seeking easy profit on the one hand and poisoning the minds of the new generation on the other.

"5. There are a total of five Arab secondary schools in Israel, only one of which teaches the sciences (Nazareth) . . . The adverse policy of the government as regards Arab culture seeks

---

Democratic Magazine, published by the Israeli "Third Force," alluded to this in its issue of September 14, 1964.

to obliterate all ties between the new generation and their distinguished past and to suppress all their nationalist feelings and aspirations for a brighter future.

"In fact, the government offers them two alternatives, one more bitter than the other: emigration or total absorption!"

This extract from the memorandum submitted by Al-Ard, dealing with the situation of Arab education, does not merely summarize the fascist means employed by Israel to wipe out Arab cultural consciousness and identity, but also sheds light on Arab steadfastness and the struggle to foil this conspiracy.

This question has been a major concern for the Arabs in occupied Palestine, and their determination to foil this Israeli policy of the deliberate production of ignorance and denial of education is what drives M. Asaf to write:[12] "While the new Arab generation is exposed to anti-Israeli influences, the older generation remains attached to the past, and the two generations are in daily contact with the Arab states and the refugees through radio and television."

Nevertheless, Israel intentionally persists in denying Arabs the right to education. It is well known, for instance, that several science faculties in Israeli universities are wholly off-limits to Arab students, a fact that drives Muhammad Dasuqi to affirm: "We cannot expect anything of value from Arab education in Israel," noting the lack of textbooks, educational supplies, and qualified teachers, as well as the existence of discrimination between Arab and Jewish students in higher education.[13]

---

12 Gotthelf (ed.), *Israel Today*, p. 47.

13 Ibid.

Following the Israeli occupation of Arab lands in June 1967, a Palestinian educator in the West Bank made the following observation:[14] "After a career lasting a quarter of a century in education, I allow myself to state that the standard of Arab schools in Israel is very low indeed and the curriculum being taught is trivial. I asked a relative of mine to bring me some books being taught in Arab schools in Israel, examined the dossiers concerned, and based my opinion on that. What is being taught to Arab students is a type of deliberate creation of ignorance (especially as regards Arabic literature and Arab history), and we would not accept these curricula here."

From that same source comes an observation made by a teacher in Arab Jerusalem who affirms: "If Israel believes it to be its duty to teach its students Zionist history, we are not obliged to do so . . . I have examined parts of that curriculum, and I believe I would be a traitor to my national convictions and to my people if I taught that curriculum."

This fact, the deliberate plan to create ignorance, aims at entrenching a colonialism of displacement, which in turn engenders other Israeli means of repression. This is evident in measures such as crippling the Arab teaching system, driving teachers away, preventing them from working, and holding a whip over their heads.

In March 1967, an Israeli named Gadish, who oversaw Arab education in Israel, delivered a lecture to the Haifa Teachers' Association and directly warned "senior teachers" summoned to hear him that "senior teachers should not regard themselves as being firmly fixed in place, like metal nails without their

---

14 *Haolam Hazeh*, no. 42 (July 1967).

heads. I shall create heads for these nails and if I can't, I will dig around these nails and pull them out."[15]

These "senior teachers" constitute in fact a most important bridge in Arab cultural life in occupied Palestine, since they guarantee the persistence of Arab consciousness and identity and are familiar with the curricula in existence before Israel's occupation. As such, they represent a problem for Israel, compared by Gadish above to nails without heads, impossible to pull out or dislodge.

Naturally, the Israeli authorities are not content with the "negative" means they employ to uproot Arab culture but also resort to more "positive" means to accompany that strategy. This manifests itself in the attempt by these authorities to poison Palestinian Arab society with a sort of phony and frivolous culture aimed at inducing Arabs to lose faith in the values, history, and future of their own culture.

Thus, in January 1961, an Arabic leaflet was distributed in Israel, prepared by Arab communists, which accused the Arab Book Company, run by the United Israeli Workers Party (Mapam), of intending to market, "without regard to cost, magazines and books that have no aim but to flood our young generation with ideas propagating anarchic and nihilistic conceptions of nationalism."[16]

In that same month, an Israeli named Moshe Piamenta delivered a lecture at the Hebrew University in Jerusalem, entitled "Language and Style in Modern Arabic Literature." In that lecture, he repeatedly advocated the use of colloquial

---

15 *Al-Ghadd* (an Arabic monthly published by the Communist Party), no. 2 (March 1967).

16 *Al-Fajr* (a literary and political monthly once published by Mapam, which ceased publication in 1962), no. 2, year 3 (February 1961).

Arabic in literary works and the abandonment and effacement of modern standard Arabic (*fusha*).[17] This was simply an extension of an ongoing and deliberate strategy. This was exposed by Jamal Qa`war, a writer and poet from occupied Palestine, who stated: "Whenever the Israeli authorities attempt to get their cronies to produce some sort of literature, they are faced by Arab refusal to countenance this plan, because its content is far removed from any Arab aspirations in this land, spreading a spirit of nihilism among the Arab masses and stifling any progressive ideas."[18]

This silent but terrifying conflict cannot end here, and that is the sole explanation for the acts of oppression, arrest, forced confinement, and occasional murder to which the educated younger generation in occupied Palestine is subjected.

Thus, on January 27, 1967, Israeli soldiers killed a twenty-eight-year-old Palestinian called Muhammad Khalil al-Zu`bi from the village of Sulam in the Nazareth district of occupied Palestine. "He had completed his secondary education some ten years earlier and had spent these years looking for work but without success . . . as is the case with most Arab graduates."[19] Al-Zu`bi was killed by an Israeli patrol

17 Piamenta was forcefully challenged by Fawzi al-Asmar, who argued that his call for the use of colloquial Arabic was a deliberate attempt at undermining Arabic culture. See *Al-Fajr*, pp. 6–7.

18 *Haolam Hazeh*, no. 36 (March 1967).

19 Ibid. Another example: at the end of 1961, the Israelis killed five Arab youths, the oldest no older than eighteen years of age, as they tried to cross the border into Gaza, in an attempt to continue their education. They included Raymond Hanna, George Nasir Shamma, and Jiryis Badin from Wadi al-Nisnas in Haifa, and Fayiz Ahmad al-Sab' from Sakhnin.

while attempting to cross the border into Gaza, but "no official statement was ever issued regarding that incident."[20]

A petition was submitted to a court of law by M. Stein, head of "The Third Force," which, as expected, was ignored by the court, and the case was filed away. The petition stated:

> As you know, your honors [this is addressed to the judges in the court], various forms of discrimination are employed against the Arabs in this country. Those who feel it most keenly are the educated classes because all government and public offices are closed to them . . . so it is not surprising if a young Arab man, having lost all hope of leading a decent life, attempts to cross into any Arab country even if this involves violating both the laws of this country and those of the Arab countries.[21]

Acts of murder of this kind, it is clear, occur repeatedly in one form or another and are reported under one headline or another. A mere glance at ordinary news reports can only raise further suspicions. Arab readers still remember a news item that reported the death of a young Arab student "who jumped from a train near the border with Jordan while on vacation from his university and fell under the wheels and was killed!"[22]

---

20 Ibid. It seems that attempts of this kind are often repeated in the same manner, because the news report used the phrase "another Arab youth killed." He was obviously not carrying a weapon.

21 Ibid. See also *The Democratic Magazine* (Tel Aviv), March 12, 1967.

22 His name was Badran Jamil Mash`al, from the town of Shafa `Amr. The incident took place in December 1965. It was later revealed that he was a member of the Arab Unity Movement, a secret student organization. It was stated that he had been savagely tortured before the alleged "accident": see the full story in the "Palestine Supplement" of the Beirut newspaper *Al-Muharrir* in its issue of January 13, 1966.

Violence and acts of terror are not confined to such incidents, and no further examples are needed to establish this. Anyone who reads the Israeli press can find all the evidence they need hidden in various places in that press. For instance:

> When a twenty-one-year-old university student named Yusuf ʿAzizi woke up one morning to study for his exams, he found a threatening note sent by a secret organization whose members styled it "Sh. Sh." Yusuf, from the village of Kfar Kina, was at the time living in a student dormitory on the campus of the Hebrew University of Jerusalem. The message demanded that he write his name in Hebrew, alongside Arabic, on the name tag on his door, or else . . .
>
> The members of that organization described themselves as having a long reach and savage means, and Yusuf was given one day to comply or else . . .[23]

This may appear like an ordinary news item if we do not follow up the fate of the complaint submitted by Yusuf to the university administration and to the police and the total neglect it was met with, as well as the procrastination and deceit that accompanied this. The head of police investigations promised him that he would pursue the matter but gave him a fake phone number, while the director of university housing threatened to expel him if he went to the police.

In the end, what lends this story significance is that Yusuf was forced to leave his university dormitory room despite all the complaints he had submitted.

It is easy to conclude from this incident that a university student was only forced to interrupt his studies because he

---

23 *Haolam Hazeh*, no. 42 (September 1967).

knew that "previous experiences" had demonstrated the seriousness of such cases and the dangers involved.

The psychological, economic, political, and physical warfare waged by the Israeli authorities on Arab culture and Arab intellectuals has had the most notable effect in galvanizing Arab literary production in occupied Palestine in the form in which we find it today. This often involves the resort to symbols and symbolism, to avoid the fate of those "found in more than one prison and the dismissal of more than one Arab teacher."[24]

This repression reached its ugliest, broadest, and most brutal dimensions in June 1967, when hundreds of Arab intellectuals received orders confining them to their places of residence[25] based upon Article 109 of the Israeli Emergency Law, which has been applied against Arabs since 1948 and right up to the present day. Since Article 109 is a daily reality in the life of Arabs under occupation, it is worth citing it to further clarify the situation:

Article 109:

I. The military commander is authorized to issue an order directed at any person as regards all or some of the following objectives:

a. To ensure, except in cases specified by the order or authorities or a person as set out in the order, that a particular person is not permitted to be in any region of Israel, as specified by the order.

b. To require that person to inform the authorities or person as specified by the order of all his movements and their timing.

---

24 Ibid., no. 36 (March 1967).

25 Ibid., no. 42 (September 1967).

c. To prohibit or restrict the use of any instrument by any person as specified in the order.
d. To impose on him any restrictions as specified in the order as regards his profession, place of work, contacts with others, or as regards his other acts that pertain to the spreading of news or advocating opinions.

Without doubt, such a law would not be applied even in the most racist or fascist country in the world, and yet a further reading of it is necessary, since its aim is not the preservation of alleged security but an attempt to completely cancel a human being.

This article is an essential part of Arab life in the occupied territories, especially the life of intellectuals. It is rare to hear of an Arab literary figure, writer, or poet in Israel who has not received such an order at one time or another. Thus, in June 1967, at a time when tens of Arab intellectuals in Israel were receiving these orders, in addition to hundreds of prominent Arab nationalists, Israeli police patrols were rounding up scores of Arab literary figures and poets in occupied Palestine and throwing them in prisons.

Among those imprisoned in early June 1967 were Mansur Kardush, Salih Baransi,[26] Fakhri Judayy, the poet Habib Qahwaji,[27] the poet Samih al-Qasim, the poet Mahmoud Darwish,

---

26 Baransi was born in the village of al-Tayybeh in 1929, and studied at Al-Nahda College in Jerusalem, where he completed his secondary education in 1947. He was among the young men who founded the Al-Ard movement and was for many years pursued by the occupation authorities. He was jailed many times and now lives "in exile" in Israel and under house arrest. He is the author of several bold and forthright articles.

27 Qahwaji is from Acre and one of the founders of the Al-Ard movement. He recited several poems during festivals that display a bold Arab awareness. He was

the poet Salim Jubran, the poet Tawfiq Zayyad, the lawyer and writer Sabri Jiryis (author of *The Arabs in Israel*), 'Abd al-Hafiz Darawshah, the literary figure Farah Nur Salman, 'Ali Rafi', Muhammad Khas, 'Ali 'Ashur, the university student Khalil Tu'mah,[28] Muhammad Rayyan, Zahi Karkabi, Mun'im Jarjura, Nasri al-Murr, George Gharib, Fu'ad Khuri, and others.[29] When some of them were released later, they received orders from the military commander confining them to their places of residence or placing them under house arrest!

Thus, Salih Baransi received another house arrest order whereby he was "not permitted to leave his house in Tayybeh between one hour after sunset and one hour after sunrise, and must, in conformity with this order, confirm his presence once a day at the police station in his town . . . Baransi had received that same order two years earlier, and the order is renewed every three months."[30]

House arrest orders were also renewed for a large number of Arab intellectuals and literary figures in occupied Palestine, including the poet Mahmoud Dasuqi, Saliba Khamis, the poet Salim Jubran, 'Uthman Abu Ras, Zahi Karkabi, 'Abd

---

pursued and jailed and remained in exile for a time and under house arrest. He and his wife were illegally arrested in June 1967, and his detention lasted, without any reason being given, until early June 1968. He was then given the choice of being stripped of his Israeli passport and expelled from the country, or else remaining in prison "until a final solution is found for the problem of Palestine." He opted for expulsion and currently lives outside Israel with his wife.

28 Tu'mah became a prominent Arab nationalist intellectual in occupied Palestine. He was recently arrested and charged with giving refuge in his house to the prominent militant Ahmad Khalifa. He had been arrested before, during the aggression of June 5. He was then a student at the Faculty of Law of the Hebrew University and secretary general of the Arab Student Society at that university.

29 *Haolam Hazeh*, no. 40 (July 1967).

30 Ibid., no. 41 (August 1967).

al-`Aziz Abu Usba`, Hisham Hafiz Ajara, "and hundreds of others."[31]

These arrests are nothing new, as is evident in the case of Baransi. For instance, we know that Mansur Kardush and Habib Qahwaji have lived in the villages to which they were deported, in exile and under house arrest, for the last three years at least.

These arrests and detentions were accompanied by wholesale acts of violence, beatings, and torture, which are a complement to the larger strategy. Thus, "two days after war broke out (on June 7), a police vehicle patrolled the streets of the village of Tayybeh, carried away some young men to the police station where they were made to enter a room, on the door of which was written 'The Discipline Room.' In that room, they were insulted and beaten thoroughly, with no reasons given . . . It has now been established beyond any doubt that those who tortured them were policemen and some civilians who belonged to another service branch,"[32] by which was meant military intelligence.

A young man named Khalil Tu`mah described in a detailed statement what happened to him at a detention camp in early June 1967. This exemplifies what happened to Arab writers and intellectuals arrested during that same period:

> I was ordered to leave Jerusalem while preparing for my end-of-year exams and to proceed to my village, al-Ramah. On June 5, while listening to the 10 o'clock news bulletin, a sergeant known to us as "Abu Surur," identification number

---

31 Ibid.

32 Ibid.

> 13225, entered carrying an Uzi submachine gun and ordered me to go with him to the police station at Karmiel, where they locked me up in accordance with Article 111. They took away my address book and suddenly I heard a voice saying: "Ha, these are Nasser's addresses! We shall send you to him straightaway! Your [plural] end has come, and we shall reap and harvest you just as our aircraft are doing from Qantara to Suez."
>
> For two whole days Abu Surur continued to insult me, repeating: "I want to drink a cup of your blood," adding: "These bestial professors who teach you how to hate the state . . . that filthy man Martin Buber!"
>
> They then took me to the Acre Police station and, as we entered, Abu Surur said to some policemen sitting there: "Look at this intellectual who studies medicine in order to poison the water in Israel!" He concluded by punching me hard in the face, an act that triggered the others, around ten in number, to attack me, punching and kicking me until I started bleeding and lost consciousness. Even so, I woke up to find Abu Surur kicking me with his boot all over my body, and the bruises from that beating can still be clearly seen on my body until now.[33]

This "official torture" was accompanied by a series of "popular attacks." Thus, the Jews of Netanya almost killed Qasim `Abd al-Qadir, headmaster of the Abu Rabi`a School in the Naqab, when they captured him on the street.[34] That city (Bi'r al-Sab`) remained closed to Arabs (especially the inhabitants of the

---

33 Ibid.

34 Ibid.

towns of Tayybeh and Qulunsuwa who worked there) for several months after that incident.

Perhaps what happened to the poet Habib Qahwaji is symptomatic of what is happening to Arab intellectuals in occupied Palestine. He was arrested on June 5 and charged with "espionage." Some months later, his wife was also arrested and similarly charged. However, "the Israeli authorities suggested to husband and wife that if they confessed they would be permitted to leave the country, a suggestion they firmly rejected."[35]

When their trial was due to begin, their lawyer was astonished to find that they had not turned up. "After contacting the police, he was told that their arrest was extended for a further three months in accordance with administrative detention regulations."[36]

Husband and wife then submitted a complaint to the consultative committee in charge of administrative detentions citing their "barbaric treatment,"[37] but were nevertheless not permitted to see their lawyer before that committee was to meet, which in any case changed nothing[38] when it did meet.

An Arab writer under occupation faces this problem in a double sense. Commenting on the Conference of Hebrew Writers held in occupied Jerusalem on April 17, 1968, the Arab poet Samih al-Qasim wrote: "In his opening remarks, the doyen of Hebrew writers, Yehuda Burla, stated: 'Israel's writers strive to deepen national consciousness and human values among youth and among the population.' Our joy at hearing this declaration did not last long because he

35 Ibid.

36 Ibid.

37 Ibid, no. 42 (September 1967).

38 Ibid.

immediately followed this up by calling for 'celebrating the glorious days that followed the Six Day War!'"

This aspect of the challenge to Arab writers is compounded by another, thus leading to a double problem. Samih al-Qasim continued:

> A conference of Hebrew literary figures is held, and we hear not one word of protest against the brutal repression to which Arab writers in that same Israel are, and continue to be, subjected. There is much talk of the trials and tribulations of "literary figures" in Russia, but as for own arrests, our being dragged handcuffed through the streets, the daily attacks upon our basic and intellectual freedoms, such as confining us to our places of residence, arresting us in our homes, censoring what we write, expelling us from our places of work, attempting to isolate us from our public in accordance with laws inherited from British imperialism . . . All these things did not merit a single word at the Conference of Hebrew Writers of the two Jerusalems![39]

This situation faced by Arab writers and intellectuals in occupied Palestine and challenged with unprecedented determination over the past twenty years of the rape of this land—has it shaken the confidence of the Arabs to the roots and clouded the horizons of their culture? Has it prevented the emergence of a literature of resistance, which nowadays glows like a beacon of hope in Arab culture as a whole?

The Arabs of occupied Palestine were from the very beginning fully aware of the dangers inherent in the struggle

---

39 *Al-Jadid* (Arabic monthly magazine in Haifa), no. 5 (May 1968).

they waged under the scourge of the Israeli military regime, and fully aware too of the strategy behind it. This is best captured in a brief but very telling observation that sums all this up: "Throughout the world, people stand on their feet, all except the Israeli military governor who stands on his tails [collaborators]!"[40]

This observation is true not merely of the political challenges facing the Arabs of occupied Palestine but also of the hidden cultural challenges that they face. Awareness of "penetration from within" to facilitate the "oppression from without" has led to the emergence of a literature that, in turn, has represented a "steadfastness from within" to facilitate "a thrust to the outside."

Arab writers of resistance literature are fully aware of these facts and of the interconnectedness of the political and the cultural. Thus: "If we do not vote for the ruling party we are disloyal to the state, and if we write a poem or story or article that expresses our bitterness we are also disloyal to the state."[41]

This in turn has led to the development of a literary style that, in essence, has adapted itself to the requirements of the "cultural war." A poet, for instance, "in order to express his true intentions will resort to symbolism . . . and poetry is a wide-open field for symbolic writing, in which the poet expresses his national consciousness without being explicit. How often have poets addressed loved ones, meaning the homeland! If a poet writes 'Woe to you, unjust person,' the authorities cannot determine his true intentions in order to charge him according to their regulations, but a subtle reader

---

40 Rashid Hussein in *Al-Fajr*, no. 2, year 3 (January–February 1961).

41 Fawzi al-Asmar in *Haolam Hazeh*, no. 36 (March 1967).

will understand the poet's real intentions and will share his feelings."[42]

The rapid emergence of a literature of resistance did not happen by accident. Nor does its importance lie in the fact that it achieved for the poetry of resistance a greater degree of aesthetic excellence than what was achieved by the short story or novel. But the fact remains that the poetry was itself the product of a deep-seated awareness of the mission of the literary figures and the intellectuals in facing the challenges before them.

Israel's daily provocations curtailed the period of artistic infancy in the occupied lands, a period spent by the contemporary Arabic literary movement in a lengthy debate regarding the extent of (political) commitment, and whether that commitment can produce original art. The massive Israeli plot against Arab culture in occupied Palestine guaranteed, by itself, a speedy end to that debate. In other words, the question of a literature of commitment was no longer a subject of debate among the vast majority of literary figures in occupied Palestine. That debate was considered a luxury accepted by no one in the face of grievous and daily challenges.

Thus, Mansur Kardush, one of the most prominent national figures in occupied Palestine, states:

> Art and culture are two weapons which, when directed at a specific objective, elevate the ideology of an entire nation. As for pure art and culture, these belong to the age of feudalism and a life of luxury and superficial prosperity. Hence, I believe that the national, social, and historic duty

42 Ibid.

of anyone who wields a pen or a brush must work toward that objective if he is to carry forward a noble message.[43]

Because Arab intellectuals in occupied Palestine realize that "there exist factors that impede the conveying of local and foreign cultures to the rest of the population, such as the impossibility of publishing and the active war being waged against the culture of commitment,"[44] they are aware that "Arab society in Israel mirrors in its behavior the larger Arab world in its conduct and reacts far more to its voices than it mirrors the Jewish society around them."[45] This has naturally led to some reliance on Arab radio stations, which "lessen the sense of loneliness among the Arabs [of Israel] and mitigate the massive burden of isolation imposed upon them."[46] These media are described as being "the point of contact between us and what has been kept out of our sight, namely, literary and cultural productions in the wider Arab world."[47] Thus, "Arab radio and TV stations have rendered us an inestimable service,"[48] to the point that they seem to have had a strong impact on much of the aesthetic output in occupied Palestine.[49]

This has, at the same time, caused a great deal of alarm and rancor among Israelis. The Israeli Sami Yakov states: "It is no exaggeration to say that the destiny of a considerable number

---

43 Ibid.

44 Ibid.

45 Muhammad Masawrah, ibid.

46 Salman Shahadi, ibid.

47 Ahmad Dasuqi, ibid.

48 Fawzi al-Asmar, ibid.

49 *Al-Fajr*, no. 3 (May 1967), where there is a heated exchange between Fathi al-Furani and Jamal Qi`war, in which the latter accuses the former of using a large number of terms in his stories "derived from Arab broadcasts."

of Arabs has been decided by the effect of these media upon their feelings and minds. This requires the establishment of a broad strategy aimed at redirecting the young generation toward the right path in order to render it impervious to the effect of certain currents of thought that are not at all in its best interest."[50]

Though they might at first glance appear to be insignificant and transient, the use made of such phenomena, seen in the context of the prior awareness among Arab intellectuals under occupation, has led to the emergence of a committed literary movement, which has come to be one of the most remarkable examples of the courageous literature of resistance in modern history.

We shall shortly see how all this has given birth to two concomitant aspects of the Palestinian literature of resistance, which together constitute the most salient and lasting characteristic of that literature: its steadfast local aspect and its Arab aspect, the latter of which has immensely enriched the course of Arabic literature. This literature of resistance considers itself to be, despite all forms of repression and states of siege and isolation, an essential part of the larger world of Arabic literature.

In any case, we have a highly important and noteworthy example that, as we shall see, reflects a great deal of what we intend.

At the beginning of 1967, the magazine *Haolam Hazeh* (*This World*) organized a workshop under the title "The Calamities of Arab Society in Israel." One session was devoted

50 *Haolam Hazeh*, no. 39 (June 1967).

to a discussion of "the backwardness of Arab society in Israel" and called upon Arab intellectuals to express their views as to the causes of that backwardness.

The editor of that magazine, having received several responses, admitted that "we heard not a single word of praise, but rather criticism and attacks. The basic thrust in all these attacks was, 'What business do you have in broaching this subject?,' while others accused us by charging that the purpose of these sessions . . . was to insult Arab society in Israel . . . and to distract the Arabs with marginal issues and side battles."[51]

Most Arab intellectuals seized the opportunity provided by that workshop to express their profound awareness of the true nature of the plight that they were enduring and against which they were rebelling. The great majority of Arab intellectuals who participated in that workshop rejected the Israeli interpretation of "Arab backwardness," since progress is not measured by "the criteria of free love and sexuality, such as a boy and girl sitting together in a cinema."[52] Most intellectuals interpreted the issue of progress and backwardness in the context of a struggle with profound dimensions, rejecting the Israeli view that progress implied and justified the enslavement of "backward" peoples.

As a matter of fact, the views expressed by these intellectuals were like the fertile soil that nurtured the seeds of the literature of resistance in occupied Palestine, embraced that literature, and endowed it with a sort of immunity that later generated self-confidence and boundless future horizons. This

---

51 Ibid., no. 38 (May 1967).

52 Edward Tu`mah `Isa, ibid.

in turn has shown that a conscious sense of commitment was able to shatter that superficial and crude Israeli deceit, and to undermine the chances of the Israeli definition of "progress" to co-opt and assimilate the Arab cultural movement.

This is an issue of surpassing importance and gravity. Thus, we know that in many developing countries intellectuals opened their eyes to find themselves engulfed by a flashy foreign culture, which was intent, through diverse means, both intellectual and artistic, upon imposing an imported way of life. There is little doubt that many of these intellectuals, caught between their local roots and the glamor of Western culture, shed these roots and loyalties, and adopted another manner of living.

The Arab intellectual in occupied Palestine faced that same challenge, but on a more widespread and harsher basis. This challenge continues to assume the form of a daily and present reality, armed with repression and seduction at the same time. The Arab writer in Israel, typically a youth with roots in the countryside, came face to face with dominant western progress and the glamor of European thought and ways of life. This was not simply encountered in the pages of a magazine, on the cinema screen, or in a book, but in the details of a daily life he was leading, hour by hour.

This is why that challenge was more serious and potent for the Arab intellectuals in Israel than it was for almost any other intellectuals in the developing world. For Arab intellectuals, Israeli "progress" was a sort of trap set in the path of their daily life, a trap that was both mental and material, which shadowed their every step, ready to snap shut.

Accordingly, raising the subject of "Israeli progress," as contrasted with "Arab backwardness," has always been a grave and threatening matter. That subject was clearly the most potent Israeli weapon—over and above repression and terror—aimed at co-opting Arab intellectuals and enticing them to adopt, willingly, an Israeli way of life.

However, what is truly astonishing is that the vast majority of Arab intellectuals in occupied Palestine, when asked for their views on this issue, gave voice to a high degree of consciousness and responsibility dictated to them by their deep commitment to their foremost and pre-eminent cause. Events were later to prove the correctness of their principled stand for the Arabs under occupation, even from the formal point of view. Following the war of aggression in 1967, "that fascist idea that insisted on describing the Arabs as backward was shattered. Shattered too was the Zionist myth that alleged that the Arabs in Israel had a higher standard of living than any other Arabs in Arab countries, rendering them like a mere shop window for external consumption . . . All that collapsed with the speed of lightning when we saw first-hand the standards of life in the West Bank and Gaza Strip."[53]

The Israeli manipulators of this Zionist strategy were doubtless shocked by the sorts of responses they received from Arab intellectuals in Israel who had participated in the poll conducted by *Haolam Hazeh* on the issue of "the backwardness of Arab society when contrasted with Jewish society in Israel and its advancement when contrasted with other societies in the Arab world."

We ought to be alert to the alarming trap set in this illogical equation, not because it was posed in the form of a question addressed to Arab intellectuals, but rather because it is one of

53 *Haolam Hazeh*, no. 41 (August 1967).

the most important constituents of the Israeli assault on Arab culture in occupied Palestine. The mere existence of this equation, irrespective of the degree of deception involved in it, and its practical implementation over twenty years of occupation, are a clear indication of the severity of the struggle in which Arab intellectuals are engaged. This in turn reveals the real value and import of the literature of resistance, which, when judged against these facts, acquires added standing and prominence.

In this regard, it would be useful to select some typical examples of the responses given by Arab intellectuals to this complex question. Below, we shall cite the major portion of the response given by the historian Bulos Farah, from Haifa, who, as we shall notice, cleverly exploited the opportunity of the survey to attack various aspects of the Israeli policy of repression, and boldly expresses his views on many issues about which Arab voices could not be heard in other contexts. Thus, his remarks are a valuable historical document and a true landmark in the history of the Arab cultural struggle in occupied Palestine.

Bulos Farah[54] states:

> How can we be expected to deal with this issue when we live in total isolation, without a newspaper, without a book, a report, or a library, wherein we can undertake studies and careful research, and draw comparisons so that our statements

---

54 Bulos Farah is a Palestinian historian from Haifa who is widely known, since he belongs to a generation that spans the pre- and post-Nakba periods. He has taught many students and has a leftist outlook. He is very forthright and bold in his views and his political and historical writings are distinguished by their powerful logic, clarity, and courage.

and writings can acquire credibility, exactitude, and scientific accuracy? That is, provided we grant that the subject is indeed scientific and not mere babbling or an exercise in smug intellectual luxury.

"In addition, a reader is surely entitled to understand the exact definition of terms like social advancement and backwardness. By what criteria should we judge them? Are these criteria moral, behavioral, cultural, or philosophical? Or [do they represent] the attempt to bring about the happiness of every single human being? How does this happiness come about? Through the public or the private ownership of the means of production? Or some idea that involves human destiny? [A] call for peace or for war? Do [they] advocate racism and discrimination or human fraternity and equality? Do [they] come about by appropriating another people's basic rights or by granting them these rights?

"In the course of the debate among the participants in that workshop, it was noticeable that social progress and social advancement meant that a village boy would come to the city and adopt its ways, shedding his traditional dress for a Western suit and playing cards in a city café. It meant that a young man from Nazareth might want to take his girlfriend to the cinema, and if he were forbidden from doing so, 'this would be backwardness,' according to Mr. Shalom Cohen!

"As for a young fellow called Muhammad Masawrah, he decided with the stroke of a pen that 'Arab society [in Israel] is backward in its thinking and its social and psychological values, and the problem in essence is cultural.' From this we are supposed to conclude that culture could either advance or regress a given society. If a society is culturally advanced, so would be its social advancement, and the opposite is true for a backward society.

"We ask: If culture is the criterion by which we measure the progress or backwardness of a society, did the German people lack culture when they closed their eyes and stilled their conscience as they sent millions to their death in ovens? Why did not the wearing of western suits, a sign of social progress according to Mr. Cohen, deter the French when they waged a war of annihilation against the people of Algeria? And why have the Americans, socially far advanced, not attempted to stop the extermination of the people of Vietnam? Or is this a matter of politics and that other a social matter?

"Who says that a person can separate political understanding from social structure? Is not the first a manifestation of social life? . . .

"Israel's policy works to retard Arab social progress in all its aspects. This is why it is resisted by the Arabs. They do not 'sacrifice social advancement on the altar of nationalist objectives,' as alleged by Mr. Cohen, but are themselves the victims of social plans . . . and here politics becomes social and economic, and vice versa.

"What do we understand by the term 'advanced society'? Does this not entail advanced social relations characterized by values that seek to bring about goodness, justice, and fairness? Where is that Jewish social advancement of which Mr. Gil`adi speaks, which displays these characteristics?

"Does toeing the imperialist line constitute social advancement? Is falsifying the general will of a minority national community during general elections a feature of social advancement? Or is it revealed by robbing Arab farmers of their lands and bestowing these lands to Jewish immigrants? Or is it revealed by paralyzing the activities of the Arab intellectual elites and the planting of agents and informers?

"The point of reference for any society is not the wearing of western clothes. The Turks took to wearing western clothes and hats, but their outward appearance has not lifted them up from the ranks of developing nations. Nor does social progress consist in allowing boys and girls to go to the cinema or have premature sexual relations . . .

"In fact, I charge whoever is responsible for drawing up the agenda of this workshop [with] attempting to evade the true conditions of the Arabs in Israel and [with] diverting our attention with marginal strife and abstract and byzantine debates about the status of women and of dowries, the advantages of western clothing, and boys accompanying girls. He omitted to mention the fact there is not a single functioning Arab cultural association throughout this country and not a single Arab organization that defends Arab rights. He failed to state that Arabs live in fear of the Israeli intelligence services and its unprincipled operatives, that there exists widespread anxiety in the country regarding the future, and that unemployment figures among Arab workers have reached unprecedented levels."[55]

Amid the challenges that have been set out briefly here, how did the literature of Palestinian resistance over the last twenty years traverse its uphill course to arrive at its present elevated

55 *Haolam Hazeh*, no. 38 (May 1967).

level?[56] What did it say? How did it express its beliefs? What level has it attained in form and content?

The following pages attempt to trace the steady progress of that literature of resistance and the forms of expression it employed, given the context outlined above regarding the unique atmosphere of repression to which the Arab intellectual has been subjected, uninterruptedly and without a single moment of relief, for the past twenty years.

---

56 For a full and detailed account of this subject, see the excellent study by Sabri Jiryis entitled *The Arabs in Israel* (1969). It was translated into Arabic by the Arab League Office, published in Arabic by the Research Center of the Palestine Liberation Organization (PLO), and translated into English by the Institute for Palestine Studies.

2

Palestinian Resistance Literature: Dimensions and Perspectives

Dimensions and Perspectives

Sami is alone on stage, in a monodrama written in occupied Palestine by a young man called Tawfiq Fayyad. He is talking about a nightmare that is tormenting him. He stops suddenly, looks at the audience, examines them with suspicion, points at them, and, in a tone of surprise, says: "What? You? Still here? What the devil are you doing here? How stupid! Did you imagine I'd leave this house to you? What nerve! What utter nerve! I almost forgot you're here, almost totally forgot. I shouldn't have. But this must never escape my mind. You occupy my house and rob me of my freedom without any justification and without being deterred by any law. Oh no! I will never forget, I promise you. Bad luck for you! But I will fulfill my promise."

His sudden exit from the play, an exit in the grip of a confusing and complex nightmare, is like an electric shock. It is a sort of revelation, like turning on the light in a dark room, suddenly converting what appears confused and complex into immediate and jolting clarity.

The play, *House of Madness*, is a landmark in the literature of resistance in occupied Palestine. In form and content, it is more than just a courageous cry. Instead, it is at once an interpretation, a perspective, and a prophecy. Sami is the lone hero in this one-man play, and the word "lone" is no mere technical extravagance in that monodrama but expresses a formal perspective, while the audience that faces him is an essential part of the play. When he stands downstage, he suddenly confronts a strange scene and says in a suspicious tone:

"Why are you looking at me like this? Why do you all assume the same shape when I look at you . . . or address you?"

Sami is a teacher of history and literature who has been expelled from his job and is living a terrifying nightmare in his tiny room. In his own soul there is total confusion, which assumes the form of madness, but when he faces his "audience," things become clear as if by magic, and the dialogue with himself becomes lucid and immediate. The immediacy here is not a weakness in aesthetic performance but a necessity that bears its own profound meaning. In the end, when he feels surrounded by those who have come to arrest him for no reason, and engulfed by a western wind and by his own nightmare, he declares: "There . . . can you hear . . . You don't scare me . . . I don't fear you . . . I will challenge you all . . . I will triumph over you . . . all of you . . . alone." Sami then exits through the door as we hear him shouting: "Alone!"

Sami is none other than the voice of resistance and the play, *House of Madness*, is nothing other than its story. He is a man isolated, besieged, pursued externally and internally, and, to a large extent, is deceived, torn apart, confused, and close to despair. Yet, in the end, he is fighting alone, unafraid, and promising never to forget. As he floats, despite himself, above the ebb and flow of humanity and its circumstances, he suddenly recovers clarity and immediacy, anchoring himself in his actual territory: "You are right! It's only natural for a criminal to be bothered by the effects of his crime! And only natural that this would drive him to commit another crime indeed, to multiply his crimes . . . so he can finally wipe out all that reminds him of his first crime!"

He understands this well and continues: "I shouldn't have bothered you with a problem that concerns me alone and bothers me! I don't know! Perhaps it does concern you too? It must concern you also. I didn't invite you into my house!"

He then points to a woman in the audience and says: "Does this problem concern you? I mean, I mean that you may be a criminal and wipe out all traces of your crime? Oh, I didn't mean, I meant that your infant might be forged by a blacksmith who then kills him? It's only natural that you don't agree."[1]

Yet this lonely individual, who alone is facing internal and external challenges, is nevertheless determined to press on with his fight to the end and is not in the least inclined to accept a partial or diminished vision. Sami, the hero of *House of Madness*, eventually arrives at an understanding of all aspects of his dilemma. Though he promises the audience that he will never forget that these people broke into his house and considers this to impose on him an urgent responsibility, he does not deceive himself by reducing his dilemma in this way. Despite his confusion and the nightmare that

1 *House of Madness* (*Bayt al-Junun*), a play by Tawfiq Fayyad. The full text can be found in the weekly supplement of *Al-Anwar* newspaper, nos. 2455 and 2461 (August 13 and 20, 1967).

weighs upon him, he is fully aware of the other dimensions of that violent act of dispossession and skillfully alludes to them, seeking to discover its local, Arab, international, and even social implications.

Through its depth of vision, the literature of resistance in occupied Palestine thus fights on more than one front. It would truly astonish any student of that literature to discover in it, in its poetry, novels, and plays, an early awareness of many aspects of the situation that Arab literary figures throughout the Arab countries have already discovered, or are about to discover, in the aftermath of the war of June 5, 1967.

In what follows we will see that the literature of resistance in occupied Palestine has succeeded in tying together the social and political dimensions of the problem, considering them to be two aspects of a theme that must inevitably be intertwined if it is to function effectively as resistance. Palestinian literature transcended that point, as it recognized early on the intrinsic connection between resisting Israeli occupation and liberation movements in both the Arab and wider worlds, waging its principled and dedicated struggle on all these fronts with all their complexities.

I chose the example of the *House of Madness* as typical of the genuine simplicity with which that process of intertwining, alluded to above, is carried out. Its lone hero, torn apart by diverse challenges, returns now and then to show that all these challenges have a single axis: direct confrontation with the more onerous Israeli challenge. Thus, all the other challenges cited are inextricably linked to that same axis, a linkage that can only serve to illuminate the dimensions of that confrontation.

This state of affairs, spontaneously gaining clarity of focus through several interconnected developments, has in turn led to a more general and noteworthy phenomenon. The vast majority of the literary figures of resistance in occupied Palestine expand and extend their commitment beyond the frontiers of art, since in one capacity or another they all belong to the national movement, are active in its various organizations, and consequently endure Israel's policy of repression. For instance, it is now widely known that the poet Mahmoud Darwish has been jailed many times and that another poet, Samih al-Qasim, has repeatedly experienced the brutality of military regulations. The Israeli government exerted persistent pressure upon a commercial company to fire an Arab employee, Fawzi al-Asmar, due to his poetry and political activism.[2] The poet Tawfiq Zayyad was dismissed from his job, as were Tawfiq Fayyad and others.

But this Israeli policy of repression has had no adverse effect on the literature of resistance. In fact, a poet like Mahmoud Darwish has immeasurably renewed his poetic vision and style while in prison, in an amazing fashion, as did Samih al-Qasim. Israeli repression, often masking itself, has attempted to splinter Arab society in Israel and to set it at loggerheads with itself, but it has led to increasing awareness of the social aspects of resistance. This was reflected especially in the short stories that dealt at first with the theme of regressive traditions within Arab society, rejecting them in order to renew the lifeblood of society and enable it to shoulder the responsibilities of continued and purposive resistance. Repression has also been reflected in the poetic output of young poets as they began to

2 *Al-Mirsad*, published in Israel, issue of June 2, 1966.

practice their craft. A close examination of that output will reveal an almost unitary observation—namely, that a young man will most often begin by rejecting the strictures of rural society regarding such matters as the relations between men and women or between fathers and sons. Their rejection, however, will rapidly assume its full and profound dimensions and lead the young person to link that rejection to the wider horizons of the diverse challenges facing Arab citizens under occupation. The end result is to lend that literature its progressive, social, Arab, and international dimensions.

When a literary critic examines the poetry of Mahmoud Darwish, Samih al-Qasim, and others, particularly their earliest attempts at writing poetry, he will note this theme clearly, since their poetry is not solely characterized by a knee-jerk rejection of specific societal traditions, but also by a surprising weakness in its aesthetic structure.

For example, in the mid-1950s, Samih al-Qasim wrote a few romantic verses about women with a noticeable narrowness of perspective and partial or weak artistry. However, within only a few years he had polished his thought and art in a remarkable manner, notably in his poem "Antigone," about the celebrated daughter of King Oedipus:

> One step, two, three.
> Proceed, proceed,
> You who are an offering to blind gods,
> You who are a sacrificial ram,
> Upon the altar of base desires of a dark age.
> One step, two, three,
> My arm entwined in yours,
> To cross that rain-soaked path.

Father!
In your face are still two eyes,
In your land are still two feet,
So travel through the night,
Through the most ill-starred tragedy in human history,
Through the night,
To create a new dawn for life.
Father:
Though your eyes have been gouged by the demons of
sorrow,
I am still firmly holding your hands,
A lamp fed by the oil of faith,
And tomorrow, father, I shall restore to you,
I swear to restore to you,
What was robbed from you by the crimes of pirates,
I swear, father, in the name of God and humanity . . .
One step, two, three.
Proceed . . . proceed

Mahmoud Darwish offers us a still more explicit example of that qualitative transformation, which grew spontaneously through the actual practice of resistance. Thus, in the late 1950s, the anger of Darwish assumes the following shape, in both content and form, when complaining of the oppressive traditions that harm the girl he loves:

And the eyelids of the living slumber on,
All but sounds of weeping
From one in sorrow and in pain,
Slipping from the depths of a village house.
She is the daughter of the village elder,

Weeping and crying out in sorrow,
And the whip is blood-red.

But notice, only a few years later, the almost incredible transformation that the poet himself undergoes, moving away from a weakness in artistic expression and fractured content, and reaching toward new heights:

The palm of my hand
is now accustomed to the wounds of hope.
Shake my hand hard
and a river of songs will flow forth.
Mother of my colt and sword . . .
Your hands rest on my forehead,
two crowns of grandeur.
If I bow my head,
a hill will bow, and a sky will vanish,
and no more will I deserve
a kiss or a prayer,
and the door will be firmly bolted
in my face.
Upon your hands
an infancy of a future is praying,
and behind your eyelids
my child is saying:
"My day is lovelier,
and you are my sun and my shade."

This process of poetic transformation has almost become the rule, and Rashid Hussein develops his own voice within that rule. In a poem dating to the late 1950s, he flirts with his girlfriend as follows:

We walk one day through your estates
and come upon a hired hand, in filthy clothes,
and you spit on the ground.
I feel a hurricane in my eyes,
a flaming fire in my body, and I say:
You there, princess!
All my poetry is for hired hands!

A few years later, Rashid Hussein would in his turn make a leap forward in both style and content. In a poem called "Noble Horses," his anger and rejection assume the following shape:

In our villages, amidst billows of smoke,
a child will grow, as do the congratulations,
and they will say:
Your sweet boy is now the dream of pretty girls,
A groom of marriageable age,
the son of so and so.
And now a generation of grooms invades my country,
a generation of boys, grown older,
like noble horses,
their minds filled with phantoms
of gray thought.

The poet continues, describing people:

All they care about is that a wife,
will give birth to a male child,
so they can say:
"She is of proud and noble lineage,
She delivered a male child,
his face like the moon."

And they will say: "her husband is a mighty stallion,
A real man . . ."
Only for their son to sit and swat flies.

In the 1950s, we read a lot of poetry in the occupied territories that is often focused on a narrow aspect of the complex social reality. In this context, we encounter the names of al-Qasim, Darwish, and Hussein, together with Fahd Abu Khadra (a gifted poet of whom we no longer hear), Ahmad Hussein, `Isam `Abbasi, Ibrahim Mu'ayyad, and many others.

However, a few years later, that narrow focus would take on wider and deeper perspectives. During that early period, the Palestinian catastrophe was still very vivid, and sheer anger, assuming a tragic and astonishing form, floated to the surface, as happened in the aftermath of the war of June 5, 1967. This is when writers and poets in other Arab countries poured out their fury on narrow and partial targets, only for that fury to crystallize later around a certain perspective. There is little doubt that Mahmoud Darwish and Samih al-Qasim were the real pioneers in that process of re-examination.

For Mahmoud Darwish, resistance as direct confrontation is so clear and firm as a central goal that he makes his ideas about society uncompromisingly subservient to that goal, when it comes to his art. For Darwish, the family is itself the homeland, and so is love. This entire theme, with all its ramifications that express its true reality, flows through his poetry in a unitary and firmly fixed manner. The following extract might summarize his stance:

Hide from my ears those wearisome superstitions!
I understand mankind better than you,

so too this fertile land.
No, I have not sold my colt,
nor the flags of my fertile tragedy.

However, Darwish recognizes that this perspective is still partial and needs to be complemented, so he follows this up, in a spontaneous flow of verse, by endowing the societal dimension with a deeper significance:

And because I shoulder rocks,
and the sickness of love,
and an alien sun,
I weep!
I depart before my due time, too early.
Our lifetime is narrower than we are,
our lifetime is shorter and shorter.
Is it true that death's harvest is life?
And will I cause a harvest of bread
to appear upon hungry hands?
or sweets in the mouths of children?

He then makes a broader appeal:

Protect your ears of wheat from storms,
with foot firmly nailed.
Bring out those barriers from your hearts,
from the heart,
So how can the barriers be breached?
Take hold of the necks of these ears of wheat,
just like embracing a dagger!
Land, peasant, resolution:

Tell me: how can they be conquered?
This Trinity: how can it be conquered?

In his own special manner, Samih al-Qasim says much the same thing in his long ode entitled "Iram":

Forever along this path,
our flags have given sight to the blind,
our voice hope to the drowning.
Forever the hell of our enemy
is the paradise of the true friend.
With the ribs of our dead,
we fertilize a wasteland;
with our blood we give water
to a child buried in the ground,
and turn a field where a tree trunk is age-old,
into the bloom of youth.
And into the sinews of factories making
jams, suitcases, or clothes,
we make flow the pulse of faithful hearts.
Forever on that path,
we wilt, as the price to pay,
for that ear of wheat to joyfully deliver
its promised harvest.
We shout with tears of joy
at that festival of sacrifice:
Forever on that path,
noble brooks will always run dry,
a sacrifice for a deep river.

Both al-Qasim and Darwish have written many poems that clearly express their progressive social ideas, in this respect following in the footsteps of their pioneering teacher, Hanna Abu Hanna.

As for the short story form, this still lags behind poetry in its artistry, reach, and quantity. In it we find a greater concentration on social issues. This is very clearly evident in a short story by `Atallah Mansur entitled "Riyad Comes Home,"[3] in another entitled "A Drop of Blood" by Zaki Salim Darwish,[4] and in many other similar stories, the most notable of which is "The Chimes of Bells" by `Abd al-Rahman Muhammad Sa`id.[5] This last displays a class consciousness and is focused on a critique of social relations. Many of these short stories deal with the traditions of Arab rural life and their rejection, or else with the worsening economic situation of the Arabs in occupied Palestine.

Nonetheless, it is equally evident in these short stories, which are mostly aesthetically flawed, that they have failed to attain the level attained by poetry in occupied Palestine—namely, in being able to tie together the various challenges confronted by the resistance movement in its cultural manifestations.[6]

---

3 Only the English text is available: see *New Outlook*, an English-language monthly published in Israel, no. 43 (April 1962).

4 *Al-Fajr* magazine, no. 2 (February 1961).

5 *Al-Fajr* magazine, no. 3 (May 1962).

6 It is truly regrettable that a full study of Arabic prose literature in occupied Palestine is presently impossible. The only novel we have heard of is *The Maimed* by Tawfiq Fayyad, but getting hold of a copy has proven very difficult. There are short stories that are worthy of notice, some of which we have cited, but they are insufficient as grounds for a complete study. In this regard, there is an excellent short story entitled "Because We Love this Land," by Muhammad Naffa`, from Bayt Jinn, which was published in *Al-Jadid* (May 1968), which suggests a very promising author. In that same issue of *Al-Jadid* a reader will encounter a perceptive critic called Muhammad `Ali Taha, from Kabul (in northern Palestine). However, poetry, which is plentiful with many poets, remains the most noteworthy phenomenon. Nevertheless, we need to

The reason for this disparity is not due solely to the fact that poetry is a more entrenched aesthetic form, has a wider reach, and is particularly suited aesthetically for the purpose, but also because under the circumstances experienced by Palestinians under occupation, publishing outlets do not allow for rapid development in the short story form.

I have thus far attempted a brief survey of the social dimension in the literature of resistance. This clear separation between these various dimensions, which *in toto* constitute the literature of resistance in occupied Palestine, was resorted to here simply in order to try to survey the essential constituents of that literature, its points of origin, and its ideological structure. Nevertheless, and on a more practical level, this separation is in fact impossible, since the literature of resistance, as mentioned above, has, through a rapid and spontaneous evolution, arrived at what may be called a unified vision. The diverse and partial dimensions of that vision cannot in any way be severed except for the explicit purpose of academic research.

In essence, the literature of resistance in occupied Palestine has defined its own role. For the poets in particular, poetry is undoubtedly a weapon, while its quality and merit reside, for these poets, in its commitment to a conscious and deliberate role of resistance.

We may therefore assert that the commitment to the national cause is the broad framework that enabled the literature of

---

point to a literary work entitled "The Sextet of Six Days," which an unknown author, self-styled Abu Salam, from Nazareth, began to publish in serial form in *Al-Jadid*, beginning in March 1968. This work may simply be considered a paradigm of the resistance story and displays a truly outstanding talent. It is a landmark in Arabic prose produced in occupied Palestine at the time of writing.

resistance in occupied Palestine to move forward and assume its responsibilities without losing any of its dimensions. Regarding these dimensions, I repeat once again that, despite their multiplicity, they revolve around a single axis: the axis of confronting Israeli occupation.

From this point of departure, we will note that the poetry of resistance, for instance, unlike much of contemporary Arabic poetry, does not begin by demeaning the value of words in that bitter struggle. Rather, it is fully cognizant of the role of words, which it sanctifies and regards as an essential and indispensable responsibility.

In this context, we have already seen what Darwish wrote in the aftermath of the defeat of June 5:

> Shake my hand hard
> and a river of songs will flow forth.
> Mother of my colt and sword . . .

This deep awareness of the organic connection between mother, colt, sword, songs, and hands is a theme admirably present in the poetry of resistance in occupied Palestine. Thus, Samih al-Qasim informs his enemy:

> These dark words, Sir,
> are a nation sorrowing.
> With them I water a seedling,
> scorched by flames from your hell.
> There is nothing to hunt in this vale of tears,
> and tears are the smiles of children.
> I shall return her son to his bereaved mother,
> and return his mother to her grieving son.

Sharpen your knife, Sir, on my wounds,
for I am the sacrifice of a word.

Samih al-Qasim defines the role of his poetry and its sources of inspiration more directly here:

From dreams in a season of plenty,
from chagrin in a tragic season of drought;
from children's toys and laughter;
from tears cleansed by the spirit of a god;
from strong arms that fashioned a paradise,
a splendid call uttered upon the ruins of war;
from wounds whose rancor grows feeble
against what one people has built on the ruins of another;
from blood and pain, from my revolution,
from my green vision and the splendor of love;
from my very life and its depths, oh songs of mine,
go forth and follow every path.

Samih al-Qasim maintains this attitude until the end. In his poetry collection titled *The Blood on My Palm*, he actually insists on this:

Our poems are engraved in steel,
on wood and rock,
and our nation urges us to march,
to march till dawn.

Long before these poets' time, the poet Hanna Abu Hanna sent the following card to his friends from his prison in Acre in 1958:

Too impotent are they
to imprison my song!
Indeed, they stoked the fire of that poem,
a blazing fire that cannot be fettered
by chains or irons,
a fire, a hell for despots,
and for that gang
intent upon evil.
Tribute enough to my poems
that they disturb
the sleep of a vicious foe.
Just imagine!
A poem that causes panic
in an iron core,
a poem more potent than a prison,
ringed by troops and barriers;
more potent and more hardy
than this mass of foreign louts,
will my song forever be!

In another poem he declares:

A people am I.
What if they jail one man?
The entire people are in rebellion.
If one poet is chained,
the song will be sung by every poet.
A people we are that surge, in multitudes,
across a bridge, over a river of massacres,
and hugs a dawn streaked in light and promise.

Darwish too emphasizes the sanctity of words and their responsibility and commitment, and does so in a unique manner:

Our poems
are colorless, tasteless, voiceless,
if they do not carry the lantern
from one house to another.

In that same poem he takes another step forward:

If only these poems had been a chisel
in the hands of a toiling laborer;
If only these words had been a bomb
held in the palm of a rebel;
Or else, if only these words
had been a plough in a farmer's hand,
a shirt, a door or a key!

Another poet states:

If my poems please my friends
and displease my foes,
then I am indeed a poet!
And I shall sing!

In another poem about Lorca, Darwish writes:

Such is a poet:
an earthquake, a flood,
a hurricane when he roars.
One road whispers to another:

A poet has walked past,
And you stones, take wing!

The poet also recognizes the cost of that responsibility:

They drove my people into exile,
and came to buy the fire in my voice.
To escape the darkness of prison,
what am I to do?
Defy that jail and its jailer!
The sweetness of faith,
dissolves the bitterness of colocynth.

But the poet knows more than this:

They tightened my fetters,
and took away my notebooks and cigarettes.
They placed dust in my mouth,
for poetry is the heart's blood,
the salt in bread,
and water in the eye.
It is written with fingernails,
with screaming throats,
with daggers.
I shall say it now:
In that detention room,
in the bathroom,
in the stables,
and beneath the whiplash,
beneath the fetters,
beneath those vicious chains,

a million little birds
will settle on the branches of my heart,
to compose a militant tune.

Knowing the value of the voice, the poet holds it as tightly as he holds his weapon:

One day my voice cried out:
I am not afraid!
Whip it if you can,
and chase its echo, as long as it declares:
I am not afraid!

The literature of resistance is replete with such explicit expressions of a mission that brooks no compromise or attenuation. Fawzi al-Asmar gives voice to a similar attitude in a poem entitled "The Ancient Temple":

In my ancient temple, I have not ceased
to gather words together,
and melt them in a flaming forge,
and mold them into a tune,
for a song of solace and hope.
Its melody will come
from our fire's melody and our great love,
from the light that shines in our hearts,
from our wounds,
wounds that lend color to saffron,
from the strong arms of that swarthy man
who smashes rocks,
from our bereaved land,
from the tears of springtime upon flowers.

Once again, we note the contents of that general framework that I have called commitment. We shall now see in the three selected examples below how poets insist upon the two dimensions of their resistance, the social and the political, considering this to be a commitment to the homeland and to liberation, through recognizing the importance of resistance and not underestimating it or treating it as mere luxury.

The poets of resistance in occupied Palestine go even further in exercising their responsibilities, as summarized for us here by Samih al-Qasim in a poem entitled "Postcard to Najib Mahfuz":

> So fill your bucket deep from that virgin well,
> and give water to the worker, baker, and Children of the
> Alley,
> for people are thirsty!
> Write about the kindling of hope,
> about the dreams of a nation.
> Blessed is that lofty word
> that shines like a lighthouse in the dark,
> and damned be those toppling ivory towers.

Thus, commitment is no mere abstract theory, nor just a question of liberation. That clarity of vision as regards the two issues, the social and the political, and their true dimensions as fundamental principles and as messages to be communicated, brooks no vagueness, ambiguity, or compromise for the writers of resistance in occupied Palestine. This is precisely what has made the Palestinian literature of resistance in the last decade a literature that neither wails nor weeps, neither surrenders nor despairs, and neither contradicts itself nor passes through periods of nervous convulsions and tremors that result from some faulty consciousness of the true nature of its circumstances. For its vision is born not of emotional improvisation but of a deep and responsible awareness of the implications of the battle in the very midst of which it finds itself. Hence, that literature has avoided the frequent romantic setbacks to be seen in most Arabic poetry of this period, which we often find to be growing more intense, and characterized by wailing, hysteria, and disengagement, the further the poet withdraws from recognition of his commitments.

In contrast to what we have all read of Arabic poetry in recent years, Tawfiq Zayyad encounters the catastrophe of June 5, 1967, in a poem thus:

> My country! Yesterday we were not floating on shallows,
> and so today we will not drown in shallows!

With that same steadfastness, Tawfiq Zayyad writes that wonderful poem called "Some Words about the Aggression." It is a poem full of sorrow, but a sorrow that is fully conscious and cannot be erased:

> You build for the present day,
> but I build high my future.
> We are deeper than the sea,
> loftier than the lanterns of heaven.
> Within us is a vitality of spirit
> longer than that expanse that stretches,
> in the heart of the infinite.

Likewise, Mahmoud Darwish receives the catastrophe of June 5, 1967, with unbelievable sorrow, which immediately rebounds to a new determination:

I lost a beautiful dream,
I lost the scent of the lilies,
and my night was long,
upon the fences of gardens . . .
But I never lost my way!

Suddenly, he adopts the tone of a popular colloquial chorus, as a background for his sorrow and longing, and as that unbreakable barrier upon which he stands:

Mother mine, here's a ditty of love!
Mother mine, a ditty!
The stabs of daggers I prefer,
to being ruled by the vile.

Samih al-Qasim encounters June 5, 1967, in a manner all his own, in a poem about a *fida'i*, which ends with the *fida'i* himself saying:

All you behind me,
betray not my promise!
Here are my veins:
Take them and weave from them
the banners of our rebellious progeny.

Such poetic stances could not have appeared so spontaneously had these poets not known from the start, not merely the dimensions of the struggle they eventually embraced, but also the extent, significance, and depth of commitment, which is more significant than a mere formality.

This leads us to attempt to discover yet other dimensions of that literature of resistance. We reviewed above how conscious commitment constituted the framework of these dimensions, and before that we discussed the commitment to the social dimension of resistance. Before us now lie two further dimensions: the international and the Arab.

To repeat, treating these issues as separate items serves merely to facilitate their study, though we have seen above plenty of examples where it is impossible to separate these issues from the overall stance of resistance.

On the international level, the poetry of resistance is fully aware of its commitment to world revolutions. It is those world revolutions that ultimately provide the prevalent climate in which a local revolutionary movement can grow, affecting and being affected by the wider revolutionary environment.

In reading the Palestinian literature of resistance, one is astonished at both the abundant quantity and the high quality of poems that celebrate world revolutions and just causes. The following poem by Mahmoud Darwish, entitled "Cuban Songs," typifies the essence and significance of that commitment:

> I never touched sugar cane,
> nor that verdant land.
> I never was in a fisherman's boat,
> sailing in the Caribbean Sea.
> I never struck a drop of water
> never patronized a hotel for foreigners.
> I never got drunk in Havana,
> on the sweat of the poor.

I never dipped my pen in the wounds of the wretched,
I never read Cuban poetry:
And yet, from Cuba, I cherish so many things.
The language of the revolution is a light
that all the languages of humanity can read.
The eyes of the revolution are a sun,
that rain at all weddings.
The anthem of revolution is a tune
known to all tolling bells.
The flag of Cuba is one
held high in the soul of a revolutionary
in the Aures mountains of Algeria.
The roots of revolution, wherever their branches stretch,
will grow inside the barricades,
and that blue and red and green flame
issues from a single anger,
and we shall bask in its glow . . .
Go kindle another flame,
all you people who shiver from the cold.

When we argued, above, that the various dimensions of that literature find themselves tightly rotating around the single axis of resistance, embraced by the committed intellectual, we intended this poem to epitomize that stance.

But it is not Mahmoud Darwish alone who is unwaveringly committed, in form and content, to that vital strand of resistance literature. There are numerous poems by Fawzi al-Asmar of a similar nature, the most celebrated being "I Am a Slave," addressed to the people of Africa. Samih al-Qasim has several poems about Patrice Lumumba, Africa, and Black Americans. In his long poem "Iram," there is a section entitled

"Postcards to the Field of Battle," consisting of several short poems addressed to the Black American singer Paul Robeson, to Fidel Castro, to Christophe Gbenye, and to the Viet Cong. In that poem, he hails the Viet Cong thus:

> Listen to it, shedding my whole blood.
> Listen to it in the valleys, in forests and on mountain tops.
> Listen to the shouts of free men and the guffaws of the
>   machine gun.
> Listen to the raids of those savage fascists!
> And I scream, voicelessly:
> Death to the gods of death!

We now notice an astonishing change in mood:

> I feel my fingers clench,
> and myself in a fleeting trance.
> I feel I'm lying in wait
> for the wolves, as they surge onto the battlefield.
> I pour fire upon these ghostly figures . . .
> And I cry.

And then yet another change occurs:

> He who swigs whiskey in New York bars
> He who meets a pretty woman in a café
> He who sings a song in the street
> He who ploughs and sows in America
> and who in Vietnam ploughs and sows
> He who remains in the factory
> Who remains?

O you foolish gods of death in America!
You foolish gods of death!

In that same vein we find a poem by Rashid Hussein about Asia entitled "The Land of Men in Revolt through Time without End," and another by Ibrahim Mu'ayyad called "Song of a Black Man," a poem that heralds the arrival of a gifted poet, though regrettably we know of no new works by him. Many other poems of the same kind can be found in the poetic output of Mahmoud Dasuqi, and in other poems, of great significance, by Hanna Abu Hanna that deal with Cuba and the African dawn.

This commitment to the international dimensions of the struggle has always characterized the poetry of resistance but did not weaken its commitment to the immediate nature of the conflict. Indeed, it gave it meaning, depth, and encouragement, unlike many poetic experiments undertaken recently in several Arab countries.

In this context, we ought to record that Mahmoud Darwish's first poetry collection, called *Birds without Wings*, was mostly in the form of songs celebrating African revolutions. His poems in tribute to world revolutions are crafted with admirable honesty, depth, and spontaneity. Darwish was also the poet who wrote the best Arabic elegy for García Lorca, the great Spanish revolutionary poet. Yet, despite all this, Mahmoud Darwish views the entire issue with full and conscious awareness, as in his ode entitled "On Aspirations":

Tell me not:
I wish I were a bread seller in Algeria,
to sing alongside a revolutionary.

Tell me not:
I wish I were a shepherd in Yemen,
to sing for the insurrections of time.
Tell me not:
I wish I were a waiter in a Havana café,
to sing the triumphs of the sorrowful.
Tell me not:
I wish I were a mere porter in Aswan,
to sing to the rocks.
My friend:
Our land is not sterile.
Each land has its own day of birth,
each dawn has an appointment
with a revolutionary.

Hence, we see that a conscious commitment to revolutions throughout the world acquires its true value from conscious commitment to the local revolution, and not by being a romantic theme that seeks to disengage from commitment through upstaging. This conscious awareness is one that the literature of resistance has come to express with clarity, immediacy, and decisiveness, and succeeds in putting the human dimension of resistance in its proper place, constituting both a challenge and a responsibility.

Samih al-Qasim phrases this major theme thus:

There, in the depths of Africa, are slaves,
male and female,
and the dawn with its palm,
gently strokes their sorrowing foreheads,
pouring into them light, blood, and life.

And there, in the depths of America,
are crimes, dissension, and loss of way.
A drum is beaten without respite,
for a city about to be sold,
and a black man about to be bought.
And here, on this near horizon,
and there, on that distant horizon,
earth does not complete its daily rotation,
without bringing forth a new triumph.
So carry your standard and follow that path . . .
Forever on that path.
Noble brooks will always run dry,
a sacrifice for a deep river.

But this theme assumes a different dimension, in quantity and quality, when the literature of resistance deals with one of its fundamental concerns: the Arab dimension. By its very nature, the Palestinian cause lies in the very midst of inter-Arab relations, so the poetry of resistance could be described as the mouthpiece of these interactions and as their chronicler.

No major Arab event takes place without leaving a record in the poetry of resistance as a whole. The Tripartite invasion of Egypt in 1956 was one such fundamental turning point in the history of this poetic corpus, as were the Algerian Revolution, the Yemeni Revolution, and the building of the Aswan High Dam. Here, and in this context, the Arab and societal commitments to resistance are seen to be organically and indissolubly linked.

We will find in the poem by Samih al-Qasim entitled "Postcard to the Egyptian Foreman Sayyid" a brief and sufficient illustration of what we intend:

You there, foreman Sayyid!
Build and raise high,
build me the High Dam,
and build it for yourself.
Quench the thirst of that burning rage,
and give us,
and give your people,
a glass of water,
and vegetables, flowers, and light.
You there, foreman Sayyid!
The promised date draws near,
and that village in the thirsty desert is dreaming,
and that seed in the patient furrow is dreaming.
So bury the fragments of that long-necked bottle
among the fragments of shattered boulders.
Build and raise high,
O foreman Sayyid,
in the name of the victims of the Pyramids,
and in the name of children,
build the High Dam,
you who begat the dream of generations!

This intense and conscious involvement in the mission of Sayyid the foreman leaves readers wondering whom the High Dam is being built for: for the victims of the Pyramids, or the thirsty land, or for an entire generation of Arab prisoners in occupied Palestine? This recalls a similar theme in another poem by Samih al-Qasim, this time about Sanaa in Yemen, on the morning after the revolution, where the poet sings for his desert and his future.

The same theme is noticeable in the poetry of Mahmoud Darwish. A long poem about the Aures mountains of Algeria begins as follows:

My house in the Aures was a free-for-all,
crying to high heaven for help,
morning and evening,
and the earth in my land is verdant green
from my blood,
so that strangers may drink their fill of it.

He continues:

A monster may kill a revolutionary
but the earth will breed a thousand more.
O grandeur of that wound! If we die,
the cemeteries will carry on the fight.
The blood-soaked epics in your soil
will never end with us,
until the farmer recovers his wheat,
and dances upon the threshing floors.

He adds:

Aures, our Arab Olympus,
Lord of glorious deeds!
We bred prophets upon your foothills,
And destinies.
Aures, my daily bread, and my religion,
You icon of worship for every revolutionary!

In another poem called "A Song for Men," Darwish further refines his stance:

> We shall leave our military camp,
> and our place of exile.
> We shall leave our hideouts,
> amidst the insults of our enemies:
> "Hey there, you Arab savages!"
> Yes!
> We are Arabs,
> and feel no shame.
> We know how to grip the scythe,
> and how the unarmed resist . . .
> and write the loveliest of poems!

It is worth noting here that Samih al-Qasim was the first Arab poet to sing for the revolution of the "Red Wolves" in the Yemeni Hills of Radfan when that revolt broke out, knowing full well its deep significance:

> Our columns are stirring!
> So drink from these columns
> that same cup of humiliation, many colored,
> you made us drink.
> Sharpen your knife upon a wound,
> whose streams of blood set on fire
> the lofty citadels of despotism.
> We have vowed to topple your throne's foundations,
> so gather what remains of your beaten troops,
> snakes and scorpions.
> You who covet the defeat of the "Red Wolves":

Your dark designs have only gleaned
a few of our dead.
Fate inevitable resides in our land,
ever since the sun was born,
land and fate unswerving.
You who worship fire!
That fire is still burning on the Suez Canal,
so what will you worship now?

At that same time Samih al-Qasim wrote another poem called "Bride of the Nile," where the High Dam is a symbol of struggle:

Listen to it . . . listen!
Roaring, blaring, incensed with rage,
across rainless wastes,
and in the depths of jungles:
Wake up, you sleepers,
and let us build barriers before earthquakes overtake us.
Take care . . . with these walls,
another mighty flood may overwhelm us.

But long before al-Qasim and Darwish wrote their poems, the Arab dimension was already deeply ingrained in the stance of resistance. We cite here a few verses from an old (1958) poem by a poet in occupied Palestine called `Isam `Abbasi:

Behold the Bastilles of Iraq,
stormed by vast crowds!
Baghdad, city of Harun al-Rashid!
Your deed was truly prudent [*rashid*].

In that same poem, the poet tours all the Arab countries, displaying an attitude both progressive and responsible, and free of romantic reactions or responses, which often lead to self-delusion.

Jamal Qi`war[7] has a poem about Algeria called "This Is the Road," which exhibits that same attitude clearly. In fact, the Algerian Revolution caused a new and unique outburst of poetry in occupied Palestine, giving rise to new motifs that are worthy of close consideration.

Even before that date, the poet Habib Qahwaji had sung of the Egyptian Revolution of 1952 and the Battle of 1956, thereby ushering in a new and radical turn in the poetry of resistance and directly broaching its principal concerns. In a poem about Algeria, he wrote:

> The blood of free men has not been shed in vain,
> and in the gathering gloom it is a flaming meteor,
> one held sacred by all eastern nations,
> sacrificing its youth to protect its sanctity.

He then added:

> People of Iraq, till when will you sleep,
> as despotism sharpens its fangs?
> Before you lies Algeria, where the armies of tyranny
> rain their blows upon us.

---

7 Jamal Qi`war was born in Nazareth in 1930 and now works as a teacher. He writes good poetry but is engaged in criticism. He is also believed to have written short stories. His articles and literary views have caused widespread debate in Arab cultural circles in occupied Palestine.

This direct appeal to the people of Iraq to rise in revolution, an event that in fact took place a little later, in 1958, caused the poet himself later to join in creating the Al-Ard movement, which was to play an essential role in resistance inside occupied Palestine.

During that same period, which stretched from the Egyptian Revolution of 1952 until 1960, the poetic style in the occupied territories was predominantly neoclassical, and quasi-polemical in tone, to adapt itself to that vast social, political, and cultural upheaval that rocked the entire Arab world. Simultaneously, that poetry was witnessing the process of its own growth and development.

Throughout that period, many Arab poets sang for the Algerian Revolution. In addition to the poets already cited, there exist long odes by Rashid Hussein, "Abu Iyas," Mahmoud Dasuqi, Jamal Qi`war, Hanna Abu Hanna, "Ibn al-Rama," `Isam `Abbasi, Fawzi al-Asmar, and others.[8] But there is little doubt that it was Mahmoud Dasuqi who, more than any other, dealt in the minutest detail with all Arab concerns.

The temper of that period is captured by Rashid Hussein in a poem:

> If humans do not understand, we'll make the rocks
> understand,
> that when the nations rise in revolt, they will triumph.
> The blood of Algeria, with its shrine the rising dawn,
> and its flame scorching the very heart of tyranny.

---

8 See the article about this topic by Fawzi al-Asmar in *Al-Fajr*, no. 10 (September 1960).

In a long ode entitled "Letter from an Algerian Revolutionary to His Son," Hanna Abu Hanna writes:

My son, for your sake I shouldered my weapon,
for your happiness my revolution and my struggle.
I saw my people like a flood of fire,
surging forth in that caravan of winds.
Behold! That flame shines bright in your eyes,
shines bright in my people's eyes,
rising in rebellion, eager for glory.
To liberate Algeria is why I rise,
and for your happiness is my uprising and my struggle.

However, as we have seen, the aesthetic forms of that period, expressed in polemic, did not come about at the cost of content. The experiments undertaken by the poets of resistance, through practice, succeeded in evolving their form into its contemporary figuration. Accordingly, two developments took place in form and content, doing so in total harmony and without either effacing the other, while the roots of commitment and defiance remained the essential link in that evolution.

Thus, a poet like Tawfiq Zayyad receives the news of the catastrophe of June 1967 and, with unswerving determination, declares:

Then . . . then what? I don't know,
all I know is that the earth is great with child,
and so too the years.

He adds:

> Lift your hands from my people,
> and do not feed the fire with twigs.
> How can you live on a ship
> and fight an ocean on fire?

He ends thus:

> A mere stumble this,
> and often does a man of high purpose stumble.
> It was one step back,
> for the sake of ten steps forward!

In fact, the pan-Arab theme has always been fundamental in Palestinian literature, and if the current literature of resistance displays such a dimension in its awareness and depth, it is because it has simply persevered with that historical theme. But this observation constitutes the title for another subject.

Above, first, we saw briefly how the literature of resistance has a social content, with its loyalty to the working class upon whose shoulders the resistance hangs its rifles and its destiny.[9] Second, we saw how that literature maintains that progressive social connection when it tackles its other dimensions—namely, the commitment to liberation movements throughout

---

9 It must be noted that the vast majority of Arabs under occupation, numbering more than 300,000, not counting those who inhabit the lands occupied in June 1967, are farmers. The poets who are the protagonists of resistance literature came mostly from the countryside. It is obvious that the inhabitants of the Palestinian countryside were those who, politically and nationally, were the ones who initiated the struggle and bore the greater share of its responsibilities and consequences, political, economic, and social. See Sabri Jiryis, *The Arabs in Israel.*

the world. Third, we saw how resistance literature is organically and firmly connected to its Arab dimension, without losing its clear vision of this social link, and with deep awareness of the significance, necessity, and authenticity of that dimension.

We have also seen how all these connections occur within a framework of unswerving adherence to the sanctity of the word and faith in its unshakeable importance and value for the resistance movement. Thus, resistance is far broader in meaning than mere armed resistance.

But we have also argued that these three connections, in the context of aesthetic responsibility and commitment, nevertheless rotate around a central axis: the courageous confrontation of the immediate, daily, severe, and exorbitant battle against an occupier who presses down upon the very existence of the Arabs in occupied Palestine.

So how does the literature of resistance give voice to this direct sense of responsibility? And how does it wage this battle without losing its social, Arab, and international connections?

In this regard, resistance literature is very rich. If the present circumstances, well known to everyone, prevent us from closely following that richness on all levels, what we have in hand will have to suffice as an illustration.

We saw above how Tawfiq Fayyad, in his play *House of Madness*, approaches the immediate aim of resistance in a progressive aesthetic manner, when the hero sheds his extreme disorientation during a moment of extraordinary clarity and decides at once and decisively that he will never forget, and will resist aggression alone.

We will note a similar moment of confrontation in Mahmoud Darwish, a moment of permanent consciousness, when he declares, in utter rejection of the evasion of responsibility, no matter how eloquently expressed:

> You are docile, like asphalt,
> despicable are you who hide
> behind a veil of boredom!

There is a similar moment in a poem by Samih al-Qasim:

> And I fear, I fear betrayal,
> a stab in the back by a dagger.
> But you, most precious of friends,
> you sweet-smelling line of verse,
> despite all doubts and sorrows,
> I hear, I hear, the sound of dawn's footsteps.

By means of such conscious moments that display total awareness of the reality of confrontation, Arabic poetry in occupied Palestine has come to chronicle the acts of mass resistance, turning its setbacks and its agonies into a fuel that keeps the flame alive.

In his short story called "Sand Dunes and Tears," Fawzi al-Asmar, a young writer born and bred in the town of Lydd, tells the tale of an Arab who has attempted to kill an Israeli tractor driver. For the court that tries him, the problem is that the Israeli does not know the Arab, has never met him, and has no idea why he attempted to kill him. For the Arab, however, there was both explanation and motive. He had seen from a distance that tractor driver attaching a chain to an olive tree he owned, a symbol of his family's history, and attempting to pull it up by its roots. As he advanced to kill him, he was in fact seeking to defend his honor.

The story has a surprising ending: The court retires to consider the verdict it needs to reach on the Arab. This problematic ending is in fact a clear and decisive stance. The court's verdict is of no importance whatsoever, since the essence and substance of the case are both present and determined by the story itself. So the ending is as far removed as possible from a question mark that a reader might imagine finding in the very last line. For there is no question mark in this regard, even though the poems, stories, and plays of resistance literature are replete with question marks. Yet these marks signify nothing other than what one might call "self-questioning," which is basically intended to assert that there is only a single answer.

We saw above an example of this "assertive self-questioning" in the extracts cited from Tawfiq Fayyad's *House of Madness*, the sort of questioning that does not question so much as assert that there is no other path. It is a questioning that resembles the following:

> Then . . . then what? I don't know,
> all I know is that the earth is great with child,
> and so too the years.

These lines occur in a poem by Tawfiq Zayyad entitled "Some Words about the Aggression," written in the wake of the June 1967 war. It is akin to the questions found in an elegy to the martyrs of the Kafr Qasim massacre, written in 1957:

> Are these the days of Genghis Khan,
> yawning as they wake from sleep?

Or are they the days of Hitler's armies,
surging like wild destructive beasts?

The same theme is present in another poem by Rashid Hussein, an elegy to the martyrs of the village of Sandala:

O plain of Ibn 'Amir,
do ears of wheat grow in your fields,
or bombs sown by war?
Or was it that in a time of famine,
you turned the flesh of children
into a crop that sways gently in the breeze?

Mahmoud Darwish endows this theme with decisive closure:

You visage of my grandfather!
You prophet without a smile!
From what grave have you come to me,
wearing a *qumbaz* colored red with ancient blood,
upon a boulder,
and an *abaya*,
colored like a hole in the ground?
You visage of my grandfather!
You prophet without a smile!
From what grave have you come to me,
to turn me into a poisonous statue?
The debt I bear is greater!
I never sold an inch of land,
never bowed beneath injustice,
yet they sang and danced over your grave.
Sleep on!

But I am awake, awake, awake,
till the coming of nothingness.

Yet quite apart from this partial theme that we have paused to consider because of its frequency in resistance poetry, we note a more general and important theme, one that exhibits a more advanced state of deliberate confrontation, capable of turning agony into revolutionary zeal. We have already noted this clearly in the poems of resistance written after the latest (1967) aggression, yet this theme is fundamental in dealing with personal or collective agony and culminates on the national level.

From his prison Mahmoud Darwish wrote some of his most brilliant and most hopeful odes, full of resolve and determination. In a poem that reminds us of the postcard that Hanna Abu Hanna sent from his prison in Ramla in 1958, Darwish wrote:

From the depths of prison a handful of my poems
has flown outwards, to grasp your hands,
blowing wind on fire.
To him who tightens the chains on my hands I say:
"These are the bracelets of my poems, and my resolve!"
Your glory is the size of my shoe, and the chains on my
hands
are as long as your history, braided in shame.
Each day I grow one year older in love of my homeland,
so hug me tight, as wind hugs fire.

He sings thus because he believes that:

He who sings on a cross of agony,
His wound glowing like a star,
Says to the people surrounding him:
Everything, except regret . . .
Thus did i die, standing tall,
Standing tall did i die, like a tree!

Samih al-Qasim has a poem called "Message from a Prison Camp":

Mother, it pains me so
that you sob so much
when friends pass by to ask about me . . .
But, mother, I believe,
I believe,
that the splendor of life
is being born in my prison camp.
I believe that my last visitor
will not be a bat,
dark as night, and blind.
The light of day will surely come by.

Al-Qasim also has a longer ode composed of four cantos, with the general title "Behind Bars." Current circumstances make it impossible for us to access the two central cantos, which were impounded by force by the Israeli military and their circulation prohibited. But the atmosphere of the first and last cantos confirms the argument being made here.

These are examples on a personal level. On a societal level, the poets of resistance have chronicled the daily events experienced by their captive nation. We saw above how Habib Qahwaji and Rashid Hussein recorded the massacres of Kafr Qasim and Sandala, and we have encountered other examples in the stories of Zaki Salim Darwish, 'Atallah Mansur, and Fawzi al-Asmar. In its turn, popular folk poetry also recorded daily events,[10] exposed and thwarted collaborators, and composed elegies in mourning or in hope and encouragement.[11] Mahmoud Darwish pursued the subject of refugees in a unique manner, while Samih al-Qasim composed several poems about the Kafr Qasim massacre, one of which we only know the opening line of, since the Israeli Military Administration imposed on the Arabs under occupation has prohibited the circulation of the rest of the poem. The second Kafr Qasim poem, recited before a large crowd, who had headed to that town to pay their condolences on the massacre's tenth anniversary, but were prevented from reaching the town by the Israeli army, led to a violent popular outbreak.

The Kafr Qasim massacre was a turning point in the resistance poetry of occupied Palestine, since it is rare not to find

---

10 In the occupied part of the village of Bayt Safafa, there is a folk song commonly chanted at weddings that says:

Where is the mother of all Arabs,
and why can't I see her?
Let her come forward, at her son's wedding,
so I can wish her joy.
She stands there, facing me,
and I can't speak to her.

A trill responds from the Arab side of the divided village and a duet ensues that symbolically transcends barbed wire in a unique manner. But this topic needs a separate treatment.

11 See Ghassan Kanafani, *Resistance Literature in Occupied Palestine* (Beirut: 1968).

some reference to Kafr Qasim as an emblem of permanent resistance.

Mahmoud Darwish has several poems about Kafr Qasim in his latest collection of poetry, called *At Night's End*. The ones about Kafr Qasim he calls "Flowers of Blood," in which he addresses the fifty martyrs massacred in that town on the eve of the Tripartite aggression on Egypt, and these fifty martyrs turn into fifty musical strings that the poet plays upon, to stress his resolve:

> To that singer who sings to you, upon olive branches,
> here are fifty strings.
> Your singer was once imprisoned by the wind,
> and a slave to the rain . . .
> Your singer, who repents from sleep,
> and finds solace in sleeplessness,
> shall call a rose that blooms, as you wished:
> A spark of fire!
> He shall call the grove in your eyes:
> The birth of dawn!
> He shall weep when a breeze
> passes over fifty strings.
> Alas, you fifty bloodied strings:
> How did the puddle of blood
> turn into stars and trees?
> The murderer is the one who died, my harp,
> and your singer has triumphed.

He continues:

> Kafr Qasim!
> I have returned from the dead,

> to live and sing,
> so let me borrow my voice
> from a glittering wound,
> and help me with this rancor
> that plants a boxthorn in my heart.
> I'm the scar of a wound that knows no compromise,
> and the lash of the whip holder has taught me
> to walk over my wound,
> to walk and walk and resist.

But just as Darwish in this poem returns to Kafr Qasim ten years after the massacre, so does al-Qasim return, also ten years later, to the same place in his poetry collection entitled *The Blood on My Palm*:

> And tiny flowers of a plum tree
> upon a woman's chest,
> and eyes closed,
> and wailing, sunk in the horror of that calamity,
> floating upon air,
> and I, an eagle's feather,
> tossed by gusts of sorrow and rage:
> a god who knows no compromise!
>
> The day they said: "They were killed or wounded"
> I didn't cry!
> I answered:
> "Yet another group has departed."
> From house to house I went,
> announcing the new year's crop,

and from the radio came news
of a glorious year:
"Egypt is a volcano, and the entire people
are defending Port Said. Brothers,
victory is assured . . ."
The day they said: "They fell dead or wounded,"
I yelled, tears in my eyes: "Hurrah!
And a thousand hurrahs!"
When they told me, I didn't cry,
and some days passed after the feast of the victims,
and I came . . .
And was met by your simple children,
and we recited the Fatiha.
Upon the eyes of your children,
you woman with piercing eyes,
the river has run dry,
and the dove has left my songs,
and I, O Kafr Qasim, I do not sing for death,
but for a hand that never ceased to resist!

Hanna Abu Hanna also wrote a long poem about Kafr Qasim, which he recited two years after the massacre. Here are some conspicuous excerpts:

How to condole?
And how can a bereaved nation
find solace in calamity?
Disasters have blown away its ease of mind,
and cataclysms lock it in struggle,
yet it still bears its wounds upon its chest . . .

and still contends,
while havoc follows in its footsteps,
along that bloodied path . . .
The way to condole is to stand shoulder to shoulder,
while the departed spirits of victims call out:
Let the sleeper awaken!

These poets, namely Darwish, al-Qasim, and Abu Hanna, also wrote poems about the Military Administration as a daily reality endured by the Arabs under occupation, about spies planted within Arab communities, about the lands robbed from Arab farmers, and about other daily crimes.

Al-Qasim, in particular, has a remarkable poem entitled "Karmiel," the name of a town built by Israel in the Galilee upon lands stolen from the Arab villages of Dayr al-Asad, al-Bi'na, and Nahaf, as part of a plan to Judaize the entire Galilee. Al-Qasim called this city the "City of Malice, Hunger and Skulls":

Morning and evening,
we behold its visage and the sky above,
and we smile, but not the smile of the fool,
but the smile of prophets,
challenged by a trifling executioner,
who seeks to hide the sun with the hem of his coat . . .

Tomorrow, you palaces founded upon graves,
tomorrow, you night clubs,
tomorrow, you wretched people,
this soil shall remember

that we gave it the color of blood,
and these rocks shall remember
shepherds who built it through singsong prayers,
and we too shall remember that . . .

Here's where their Book of Genesis shall end,
and where the book of our genesis shall begin!

Examples of this genre are too numerous to count, and we now possess a vast quantity of poems that need urgently to be collected in an anthology, for they constitute the most luminous and significant aspect of our current cultural life.

Resistance poetry and literature in general have always been optimistic in tone, but that optimism is not born in a void or a sort of fanciful gamble. Otherwise, it would have cracked and splintered in these last twenty years of captivity and agony. Instead, it sprang from a healthy and deep-seated consciousness of the dimensions of the battle, and from genuine commitment to the masses and their just causes, a commitment which is both the object and the means of resistance at the same time.

Hence, the poetry of resistance began from the ground of commitment and commitment to the land, and through practice and confrontation has come to reveal its depths. Despite unbelievable obstacles, it has achieved an admirable level of excellence in both content and form, placing itself at the forefront of the current literary movement in the Arab world.

Thus, the literature of resistance, having tied itself to its origins, ascertained its horizons, and committed itself to its true principles, has not shown any sign of renunciation or shirking of responsibility, nor any sign of blaming or wailing. It has played its role responsibly, refusing to hide behind a veil of boredom, or cheap upstaging, or the kind of humor that the gentlest of breezes dissipates. Resistance literature has never been a mere luxury but has ever been a commitment to arms, as well as to aesthetic and moral principles.

This alone is why Mahmoud Darwish is practically the only poet throughout the larger Arab world who faces the catastrophe of June 5, 1967, with unswerving determination, turning it into a spur for action:

> My homeland!
> My iron chains have taught me
> the violence of vultures
> and the gentleness of the optimist . . .
> I never knew that, beneath our skins,
> lies the onset of a storm,
> and the wedding of braided hairs!
> They denied me light in my prison cell,
> but in my heart there glowed
> a sun of torches.
> On the wall they wrote my identity card number,
> and along that wall
> a meadow of wheat came to sprout.
> With my teeth I drew your bloodied face,
> and wrote a song to the passing night.
> Into the flesh of darkness I plunged my defeat,
> and dug my fingernails in the poetry of light.
> Those conquerors perched on the rooftops of my homes,
> have unleashed nothing but portents of my earthquakes.
> They shall see nothing but a bright light,

shining on my forehead,
and hear nothing but the clanking of my chains.
If I burn upon the cross of my worship,
I shall become a saint,
dressed as a fighter!

3

An Anthology of Poetry, Short Stories, and Drama

Poetry

Hanna Abu Hanna[1]

A Child from My People

Dedicated to that child and his friend, one of whom raised the other on his shoulders to peek through the window of my prison cell. He peered through the darkness till he saw me, greeted me, then flung these words into my cell: "Don't be afraid of them . . . Be brave!"

1 Hanna Abu Hanna was born in 1928 in the village of al-Rina, near Nazareth, and studied at the Government Arab College in Jerusalem. He worked in education, then for the newspaper *Al-Ittihad* and the magazine *Al-Jadid*. He currently teaches Arabic literature at the Orthodox College in Haifa. He has published several critical and literary studies and is considered an educational pioneer. Most Arab poets of resistance in occupied Palestine were either his students or inspired by his poetry.

Behind the bars, and through that window,
a forehead appears,
like the crescent moon, of a child,
brightly shining, youthful,
tender like mint,
sweet smelling like basil, compassionate.
Behind the bars, a forehead appears,
and eyes that search and shine in that pitch-dark corridor,
and flutter like white wings,
scanning, determined, unswerving,
challenging the darkness and looking for signs of a
prisoner.
Behind the bars, shining eyes appear,
eyes of a child, barely ten years old,
who climbed to the window of my cell,
and peeked in, looking for me,
to pour forth hope and tenderness upon my dark horizon.

I observe him, from a corner in my cell,
I watch him, worried, and am torn by doubts:
Was it some playfulness that brought him to me,
some whim?
A child curious to know what a prisoner looks like?
Or has he been sent on some errand,
to climb in secret upon my windowsill,
like a carrier pigeon,
bringing me some glad news, some message?
(For in their struggle my people
welcomes help from its legions of children,
and sends them forth like homing pigeons,
like marching troops, ready to fight.)

You bird on my prison bars, you, olive branch,
what is it that you bring me?

Silently I watched his eyes,
as his hands gripped firmly
the green windowsill,
like the claws of a hawk, invincible,
while I watched . . . what next?
An anxious voice whispers:
"Can you see him?"
Another whisper answers, frustrated:
"No, I can't. The darkness veils him."
He turns back, gazing intently,
and a stillness falls,
and in that dark corridor,
eyes flutter and glow.

The first voice whispers again to him:
"Why can't you see him?
Climb down and lift me up on your shoulders,
my eyes can see better than yours in the dark.
Lift me, and I shall see him,
And plant your feet firmly."
Yet sorrow remained peering through the window,
challenging the darkness, looking for signs of a prisoner.

Moments pass in stillness,
where eyes begin to twinkle,
and his voice sings out in joy:
"I can see him! I can see him!
There he is, hiding in that corner,

sitting there, and deep in thought.
And on a yellow table are some newspapers,
and a bowl of soup,
and black bread, untouched,
and unlit cigarettes.
I see him smiling,
waving a pen in his right hand."

He greeted me, and I returned his greeting.
He hardened his visage,
and in a voice of magic inspiration,
carved from a luminous diamond,
his lips called out to me:
"Stand firm! Don't ever be afraid of them!
Be brave and fear no one,
and be strong in resolve,
for victory belongs to the strong in resolve."

Into that cell which held me
poured forth a flood of echoes,
a raging flood of emotions,
and upon my heart gushes
a perfumed flask, from which seeps forth
a flux of poetry.

The boy departed,
like a bird, from the windowsill.
And I grew still, lost in thought,
motionless.
And in that cell that holds me,
clamored a flood of echoes,

and sundry feelings, unruly, encircle me,
and worries.

A boy?
Rather, the generation of dawn,
and standards proclaiming victory,
and a springtime, fragrant with flowers,
that challenge evil weeds,
and sway its perfumed sleeves,
in the bitter field of calamity,
safeguarding the thorns
that will bloody the hands of oppressors.

A boy from my people . . . Hurrah!
Was he a boy?
Rather, this was but an inspiration, inspired!

Behind these bars and from a window,
a forehead appears,
and I am a nation, imprisoned,
in a corridor of suffering.
My shield is patience,
and a ten-year struggle, unceasing.
My weapon is my resolve, which I brandish
to protect my sacred land.
Imprisoned, my masses forge their unity
into a lion's den,
and repel with strength of will
the schemes of enemies.
In the darkness of that corridor,
eyes appear, shining bright,

two eyes of a dawn, and in their eyeballs
the flashing of two vultures.
The infamy of chains is shattered
by hands compassionate.
The dawn of freedom is breaking
in my fatuous jail,
stepping over its darkness, scattering it,
and leveling jails.
And upon my dark horizon shines fortitude
and certainty,
and a clamor, pouring into my heart,
a flood of echoes:
"Stand firm! Don't ever be afraid of them!
Be brave and fear no one,
and be strong in resolve,
for victory belongs to the strong in resolve!"

Mahmoud Darwish[2]

Mawwal[3]

I lost a beautiful dream,
I lost the scent of the lilies,
and my night was long,
upon the fences of gardens . . .
But I never lost my way!
The palm of my hand
is now accustomed to the wounds of hope.
Shake my hand hard
and a river of songs will flow forth.
Mother of my colt and sword:
Mother mine, here's a ditty of love!
Mother mine, a ditty!
The stabs of daggers I prefer,
to being ruled by the vile.
Your hands rest on my forehead,
two crowns of grandeur.
If I bow my head,
a hill will bow, and a sky will vanish,
and no more will I deserve
a kiss or a prayer,

---

2 Mahmoud Darwish was born in the village of al-Birwa, near Acre, in 1941. The Israelis bulldozed his village in 1949. He is a leftist and was before that a member of the Al-Ard group. He was jailed three times, in 1961, 1965, and 1967. He currently resides in Haifa under house arrest. He has published the following poetry collections: *Birds without Wings* (1960), *Olive Leaves* (1964), *A Lover from Palestine* (1966), and *Night's End* (1967), and he currently plans to publish a fifth collection entitled *Daily Diary of a Palestinian Wound.*

3 1967.

and the door will be firmly bolted
in my face.

They said: You love that pretty girl.
I said: But my love is a worship.
Hair is the most beautiful of thickets,
and chests the most precious of pillows,
and weddings are the paths of heroes!
Mother mine, here's a ditty of love!
Mother mine, a ditty!
The stabs of daggers I prefer,
to being ruled by the vile.
I lost the best part of sunrise,
but did not waste the nights.
Never mind!
My wounds are the roses of true men,
and the festival of the morning.
The breeze grows sleepy with me,
and on my forehead is a smile.
My chains are a ring of glory
and a beauty spot of dignity,
my arms ready to challenge . . .
Mother mine, here's a ditty of love!
Mother mine, a ditty!
The stabs of daggers I prefer,
to being ruled by the vile.
Upon my lips, be a name
for all the seasons.
From my hands they only robbed
the abode of fields,
but you are a world to me.

Upon your hands
an infancy of a future is praying,
and behind your eyelids
my child is saying:
"My day is lovelier,
and you are my sun and my shade."
Mother mine, here's a ditty of love!
Mother mine, a ditty!
The stabs of daggers I prefer,
to being ruled by the vile.
Is it the earth or is it you before me?
Or are you twins?
Who was it who stretched my arm to the sun:
the earth or two shining orbs?
It's all the same to me,
all the same!
If I lose my beloved
I lose the taste of ears of wheat,
and if I lose the garden,
I lose the fragrance of hair in braids,
and the true dream vanishes!
It is roses I defend,
longing for your lips.
It is the dust of streets I defend,
afraid for your feet,
and my defense it is that I defend!
Mother mine, here's a ditty of love!
Mother mine, a ditty!
The stabs of daggers I prefer,
to being ruled by the vile.

The Singer Chanted[4]

Thus do trees grow,
and pebbles dissolve,
ever so slowly,
in the ripples of the river!
The singer, on his way to the city,
is ever mindful of the truth . . .
Like mindfulness itself!
To the wind he said, in irritation:
"Destroy me as long as you're my life,
and as fate pretends to decree,
and drink me,
a toast to the triumph of a corpse."
Thus does the rain fall,
you lips of an accursed city!
They distanced him from his audience,
and from drunkards.
They tied him up and tossed him
in a detention room,
cursing his mother, and his father's mother,
and yet the singer,
sings of the hairs in autumn's sun,
and dresses wounds,
with his strings.
He who sings on a cross of agony,
his wound glowing like a star,
says to the people surrounding him:
"Everything, except regret . . ."
Thus did I die, standing tall,

---

4 1964.

standing tall did I die, like a tree!
Thus does the cross become a pulpit,
its rod a tune,
its nails strings.
Thus does the rain fall,
thus do trees grow.

The Song's Martyr[5]

They set up the cross on the wall,
and untied my chains,
while the whip was like a fan,
and the tread of boots
a tune that whistles: Sir!
And says to the dead: Beware!
"You there,"
barked a savage:
"I'll send you on your way
if you prostrate yourself twice
before my throne,
and if you humbly kiss my hand twice,
or else,
you shall mount on that wooden cross,
martyr to a song, and to a sun!"
I was not the first to bear a crown of thorns
to tell that swarthy lady: "Cry!"
O you whom I love, like my faith:
Your name on my mouth is dipped
in thirst, begrimed in dust,
the taste of wine, long aged in casks!

---

5 1964.

I was not the first to bear a crown of thorns
to say: "Cry!"
Perhaps my cross shall be
the back of a horse,
and the thorns on my forehead,
streaked with blood and sweat,
shall be a crown of laurel.
Perhaps I shall be the last to say:
"I longed for death!"

My Father[6]

Ignoring the moon,
he bent down to hug the earth
and prayed . . .
to a sky with no rain,
and forbade me from traveling!
Lightning lit up the valleys
where my father
raised stones!
Long ago this was . . . and brought trees to life.
His skin was flaked with sweat,
his hand dressed stones,
and on that distant horizon,
he wept the following song:
Odysseus was a champion.
In the house were loaves of bread,
and wine, and covers,
and horses and shoes.
Once my father said,

---

6 1964.

while praying on a stone:
"Ignore the moon and beware of the sea . . . and of travel!"
The day the god was whipping his slave
I said: People, let us blaspheme.
Lowering his arm, my father related to me:
Conversing with his torment,
Job would thank
him who created worms . . . and clouds.
He created that wound for me alone,
and not for a dead person . . . or for an idol.
Ignore the wound and the pain,
and help me to feel remorse.
A comet passed across the horizon,
descending . . . descending.
My shirt was caught
between the fire and the wind,
and my eyes contemplated
some images in the dust,
and my father once said:
"He who has no country,
has no grave in any ground . . ."
and forbade me from traveling!

Sorrow and Anger[7]

The sound on your lips brings no joy,
and the fire in your lungs does not prevail,
and your grandfather is being crucified
upon the boot of an immigrant,
and her lips are given to others,

---

7 From *Olive Leaves* (1964).

and her breasts are being milked!
So why aren't you angry?

Yesterday we met on the path of night,
and from moment to moment
your lips carried
all the soft moaning of an oak forest.
For the fiftieth time you related to me
the love of some girl and the passion of some boy,
and the bottle of brandy,
and the tents and the Yemeni sword . . .
In vain can your Arab wound grow numb
through the din of gurgling bottles!
In vain, you night canary,
can you tame defiant aspirations!
The wind on your lips
blights the songs you sang!
So why aren't you angry,
when your song, O night canary,
brings no joy?

They said: Smile so you can live.
Your eyes smiled at that road,
and your eyes disavowed a heart burnt to ashes,
and vowed to me:
I am happy, Comrade,
and have read about the true meaning
of the smiles of slaves:
Wine, greenery, and a shapely body!
But if you see my blood in your wine, Comrade,
how can you drink?

The embers in your lungs, beneath the ashes,
will stir tomorrow.
So why aren't you angry,
as long as the nature of fire in your heart
does not overspread?

The village, the ruins,
and the watchman, and a waste land,
and the stumps of your olive trees
are nests for owls or ravens!
Who has prepared the plough this year?
Who has dressed the soil?
Hey, you!
Where's your brother?
Where's your father?
Both a mirage!
Where did you come from?
From a wall?
Or did you descend from the clouds?
I wonder, will you safeguard the dignity of the dead,
and at night's end knock upon a door?
And why aren't you angry,
so long as your grandfather's flesh
is being crucified upon the boot of the night?

We bore our sorrows for years,
and morning never dawned,
and sorrow is a fire
whose flame is put out by the stream of days,
and stirred by the wind.
But the wind is yours to command . . .

So how can you hold it back
when you have no other weapon
but to face the wind and the fire,
in a homeland unfettered,
a free-for-all?

Ruba`iyyat (Quatrains)[8]

My homeland!
My love for you has granted me
nothing but the wooden planks of my cross!
Homeland, my homeland, how beautiful you are . . .
Take my eyes, my heart, my beloved!

In the coffins of my beloved, I sing
to the swings of the youngsters, I love!
My grandfather's blood is coming back to me,
so wait for me,
the end of night . . . is day.

Here is a scythe my father once used
to mow ears of wheat every summer,
and I give you to drink from a luminous star,
you age-old friend,
so mow down every wrong!

Perhaps I recall horsemen,
and a Bedouin girl named Laila,
and shepherds milking she-camels at sunset.
Ah my country! I did not long for Jahili times
for my future is better than my present and my past!

8 1964.

With his plough he cut one furrow after another.
He sowed wheat gently,
and prayed to the clouds,
and a burst of blood poured down!
They fired on him . . . did you hear it, you sleepers?

The latest news from Madrid:
The wound said,
The patient one has exhausted his patience!
At night they executed Golian,
while orange blossoms still spread their fragrance!

A Song for Men[9]

To the loveliest of riverbanks I walk,
so do not grieve for my feet
from the thorns . . .
My footsteps are like the sun,
which cannot grow strong without my blood.

To the loveliest of riverbanks I walk,
so do not grieve for my heart
from the pirates.
My heart, kneaded like the earth,
is a gentle breeze in the hand of love,
and a powder keg in the face of hatred.
To the loveliest of riverbanks I walk,
so do not grieve for my eyes
from the desert . . .
The bitterest of sorrows

9 1966.

I sweeten with the sugar of my verdant purpose,
and it turns like wine that melts in its cask!

To the loveliest of riverbanks I walk,
and when the soles of my shoes are tattered,
I lay down my eyelashes,
Yes . . . my eyelashes!
I do not long for sleep, nor do I tremble,
for the bed of those who slept
is there, in the middle of the road,
like the plank of a casket!
Come, you comrades of chains and sorrows,
and let us walk,
to the loveliest of riverbanks let us walk.
We shall not be vanquished,
and shall lose nothing
but the casket!

To the heights our throats,
to the heights our eyes,
to the heights our hopes,
to the heights our songs!
From our gallows,
and the crosses of our present and our past,
we shall fashion ladders to our promised tomorrow,
and scream: O Ridwan!
Open your locked gate!
From our throats
and from the plaints of our elegies,
shall flow forth odes . . . like sweet wine,

to be imbibed while merrymaking,
and sung in the streets,
in factories
in the quarries,
in the fields,
in our gatherings.

From our eyes we shall build
an observatory that reveals
what is furthest, deepest and most wondrous.
We shall observe nothing but the dawn,
and hear nothing but victory.
Every revolt on earth
makes us quake,
and every beautiful woman on earth
shall kiss us.
Every orchard on earth
we shall eat some fruit from,
and every ode on earth,
when it dances,
we shall hold by its waist.
Every orphan girl on earth, if she calls for help,
we shall aid.

We shall leave our military camp,
and our place of exile.
We shall leave our hideouts,
amidst the insults of our enemies:
"Hey there, you Arab savages!"
Yes!
We are Arabs,

and feel no shame.
We know how to grip the scythe,
and how the unarmed resist.
We know how to build a modern factory,
and a house,
and a hospital, and a school, and a bomb, and a rocket . . .
And music,
and write the loveliest of poems,
in sentiment, thought and elegance!

Samih al-Qasim[10]

Postcards to the Fields of Battle

I. To the Egyptian Foreman Sayyid

You there, foreman Sayyid!
Build and raise high,
build me the High Dam,
and build it for yourself.
Quench the thirst of that burning rage,
and give us,
and give your people,
a glass of water,
and vegetables, flowers, and light.
You there, foreman Sayyid!
The promised date draws near,
and that village in the thirsty desert
is dreaming,
and that seed in the patient furrow is dreaming.
So bury the fragments of that long-necked bottle

---

10 Samih al-Qasim was born in 1939 in the town of al-Zarqa in Transjordan, where his father was stationed as an army officer. The family returned to al-Rama (in Galilee) when he was a child, and he completed his primary education there, then his secondary education in Nazareth, following the Nakba. He worked as a teacher but was dismissed from his job following the publication of his second poetry collection, entitled *Songs Along Paths*, from which the censors excised several poems. He was jailed twice, in 1961 and 1967, and was put under house arrest in Haifa after leaving prison, under orders forbidding him to leave his house after 6 p.m. He also had to report his presence twice a day at a police station. He is a Muslim of the Druze faith, left leaning in politics, and very productive. In addition to his poetry collections entitled *Pageants of the Sun* (1958), *Songs Along Paths* (1964), *Iram* (1965), and *My Blood on My Palm* (1967), his latest poetry collection is called *The Smoke of Volcanoes* and was published in early 1968.

among the fragments of shattered boulders.
Build and raise high,
O foreman Sayyid,
in the name of the victims of the Pyramids,
and in the name of children,
build the High Dam,
you who begat the dream of generations!

II. To the Viet Cong Revolutionaries

Listen to it, shedding my whole blood.
Listen to it in the valleys, in forests
and on mountain tops.
Listen to the shouts of free men and the guffaws
of the machine gun.
Listen to the raids of those savage fascists!
And I scream, voicelessly:
Death to the gods of death!
I feel my fingers clench,
and myself in a fleeting trance.
I feel I'm lying in wait
for the wolves, as they surge onto the battlefield.
I pour fire upon these ghostly figures . . .
And I cry.
He who swigs whiskey in New York bars
he who meets a pretty woman in a café
he who sings a song in the street
he who ploughs and sows in America
and who in Vietnam ploughs and sows
he who remains in the factory
Who remains?
O you foolish gods of death in America!

You foolish gods of death!
Listen to them, shedding all my blood.
Listen to them in the valleys, in forests and on mountain tops:
Those evil fascists raiding!
And I scream, scream at the top of my voice:
"Death to the gods of death!"

In your eyes, you freedom-loving Viet Cong,
shines the dawn of victory!

III. To Najib Mahfuz

They lived, but not a word ensued,
they died, but not a word ensued.
For eloquence, and well-burnished sheets of paper,
and a lofty style
and expensive ink, and silver pens,
were all captive,
their charms toys to the nobles,
while simple people lived, and not a word ensued,
and died, and not a word ensued.
So fill your bucket deep from that virgin well,
and give water to the worker, baker, and Children of the Alley,
for people are thirsty!
Write about the kindling of hope,
about the dreams of a nation.
Blessed is that lofty word
that shines like a lighthouse in the dark,
and damned be those toppling ivory towers,
and those captives of the nobles!

IV. To Castro

Onwards, onwards, on this path,
you breaker of a nation's chains,
Onwards, you first of torches,
to shine in occupied American darkness.
Onwards, as long as in the house
there remain dregs of fascist thugs.
Onwards: the dawn and sugar cane
are weapons invincible.
You who succor plundered islands,
and brings solace to nations in distress:
the flags of the pirates
shall sink to the depths, the very depths,
disfigured, bloodied, vanquished,
in the name of freedom and humankind.
Onwards, onwards, you people of Cuba,
Christ is no longer on the cross!

V. To Paul Robeson

From the furthest reaches of earth,
your song is a drink of water in my house,
and in my heart makes flutter
a bird, dark-skinned, an exile.
Your song is a drink of water in my house,
you deepest of voices!
Your song is a drink of water in my house,
you hardiest of posters on this path,
you who exposed the wickedness
of man against man!
From the furthest reaches of this world comes the cry:
"For God's sake take my mother home

that she might not witness my death!"
Before my eyes swim the ghosts
of the Ku Klux Klan,
amusing themselves,
by crucifying you in the town square.
They amuse themselves
by crucifying me in the town square,
and I wake to a drumbeat,
and faith returns to my heart!

VI. To Christophe Gbenye

His fingernails are still long,
his eyes are still shooting bolts of fire.
He is still protected by the gloom
in the heart of the African jungle.
He is still making us quake
with hatred, though not with fear,
that monster who murdered Lumumba,
and Congo's river of blood still flows
on every road,
and the prayer of the Congo remains,
and the night is long and deep.
So lift your torch, burning fiercely,
and light the way for your beloved mother,
for the path is long where there is no light,
but the path is short so long as your red flag
flutters along your march.
Raise it high, and let it always billow
along the path, and over the bodies of martyrs.
The path is short!
The path is short!

Thus

As you plant a palm tree in the desert
As my mother plants a kiss on my frowning forehead
As my father takes off his abaya
and teaches my brother the alphabet
As the helmets of war are laid aside by a regiment
As a stalk of wheat raises its head from the ground
As a star smiles upon a lover
As a gentle breeze soothes the face
of a tired worker
As a factory rises high amidst the clouds
As some friends sing the prelude to a song
As a stranger smiles to another in friendship
As a bird returns to its long-sought nest
As a schoolboy carries his backpack
As the desert knows how to bloom,
Thus does Arabism pulse in my heart.

Not

One after the other,
The dead fall.
My country, defend the mast,
for the knight of the wind is returning,
is returning.

Drop after drop,
the tears fall upon the deserts.
Be of good cheer: you shall grow verdant
you plains of gloomy vision.

Yesterday was a hateful day.
It trampled us disdainfully and passed.

Tomorrow we shall not sleep
like tattered garments that stalk the land,
bringing weakness and humiliation.
I swear: our roots shall never die!
I swear: our blood shall never go unavenged!

To All Those Well-Dressed Men at the United Nations

Gentlemen, of all lands:
Your neckties at the height of noon,
and those exciting debates,
what good is all this at times like these?
Gentlemen, of all lands:
Moss has grown in my heart,
and covers all walls of glass.
These numerous meetings
and these speeches galore,
and the spies, and the statements of whores,
and voices confused,
what good is all this at times like these?

Gentlemen:
Let the wheel of fortune turn where it may,
and come!
I long for bridges in this world
and my blood is yellow.
My heart has collapsed in the mud of pledges,
You gentlemen of all lands!
Let my shame be a plague, my sorrows a serpent.
You black and shining shoes of all lands:
My rancor is louder than my voice, and our age is cowardly,
And I . . . have no hands!

Rome

Rome burnt down centuries ago,
but the root, firmly anchored in its soil,
did not lose the sense of pulse in calamity.
Nero! Rome has come back!

Karmiel[11]

"City of Malice, Hunger, and Skulls"
Morning and evening,
we behold its visage and the sky above,
and we smile, not the smile of fools,
but the smile of prophets,
challenged by a trifling executioner,
who seeks to hide the sun with the hem of his coat . . .

Tomorrow, you palaces founded upon graves,
tomorrow, you night clubs,
tomorrow, you wretched people,
this soil shall remember
that we gave it the color of blood,
and these rocks shall remember
shepherds who built it through singsong prayers,
and we too shall remember that . . .

Here's where their Book of Genesis shall end,
and where the book of our genesis shall begin!

---

11 In the early 1960s, the enemy stole the lands belonging to the Arab villages of al-Baʿna, Nahaf, and Dayr al-Asad and built upon them the Jewish town of Karmiel as part of the unceasing attempts to Judaize the Galilee.

Incantations to Protect One Against Air-Raids

We are now in the midday sun,
and half the sun's disc is weeping in the alley.
The hens are wailing at the sound
of large cleavers descending,
while my father loads meaningless bullets,
as his comrades call out insistently:
"Al-Birwa has fallen![12]
Alas that luckless town!
And the noose is tightening on Layyat!"[13]

I was a child then,
still sucking the milk of a nine-year-old
and the milk of calamity.
I was a serious child, with dreamy eyes,
surrounded by a thousand nets,
when my mother said to me, disconcerted:
"Tonight, do not take off your clothes
at sleep time,
and keep your shoes on!"
I did not understand what she meant exactly,
and I wept.

Night has now begun to make us sleepy.
The moon's half disc, betrayed, weeps in the alley.
My father has not returned yet,

---

12 Al-Birwa, an Arab village destroyed by Israel in 1949, whose ruins were then ploughed up. It is some fifteen kilometers from Acre.

13 Al-Layyat is the name of a road some three kilometers beyond al-Birwa, in the direction of Safad. The Arab Liberation Army was stationed there in 1948, near the village of Majdal al-Kurum.

and rumors abound
about treasonous leaders,
and the army surging, but in retreat,
that made us cry.

The "Liberation" Army, a flock of sheep, hurried
northwards,
and the soldiers of "Liberation" abandoned their rifles in
the trenches,
and in the mud . . .
They deck themselves with medals and battle ribbons.
Soldiers of "Liberation": a disgrace to manhood!

Children of Rama:[14] the conqueror has arrived!
And you people, the conqueror is here!
Safe is now your refuge,
and what good does it do for you now to sing
songs of pride?
Aim all your incantations against the enemy's aircraft,
and get God to aid you against them.
Fire the Ten Commandments at them,
and the Book called Jafr,
and those manifest verses from heaven!

I was a child then,
And they taught me that the earth
rotates in the palm of the sky.
They taught me that He, glory be to Him,

---

14 Al-Rama: a village on the road to Safad, famous for its olive orchards, and the poet's hometown.

grants life and death to whomsoever He wills.
They taught me to obey the saints.
They taught me hypocrisy and rope dancing,
and contempt for women.
They taught me magic and to believe in ghosts,
in incantations and in spells against evil spirits,
and to fear the night.
They taught me whatever they wished
but did not ask me what I wished.
The horse of al-Khidr will keep me safe,
and the saints shall suffice me!

My defeated father! My humiliated mother!
I shall throw to the devil what you taught me
from the teachings of the tribe!
I spurn them all, these barbaric rituals,
and pull them out by their roots,
those ludicrous customs.
I spit out my rancor and my shame
in the faces of those virtuous saints.
I kick the filth of my humiliation and defeat
towards those takiyyas and dervishes,
and dwarfs who bark when perched on elevated chairs!

From the pit of my hell, I scream:
You globs of mud,
stuck to my great historic shoe,
I sentence you to death!
So prepare a shroud,
made from skins of half-men,
and, if you wish,

an inscription, a cross, stars, and a crescent moon,
and with your hands weave all these
into devotions and prayers!

Terror, the Last Line of an Ode, and Bats

I. Terror

When the sun set, they said:
Go hide in a room of some homeland!
They said: You're forbidden to harbor these troublesome thoughts,
between myself and the moon.
It terrifies them, I know, to sow boredom,
between me and the stars.
It terrifies them when I touch the trunks of trees!
When the sun set, they said:
Go hide in my room, you homeland!
They said: If I am a stranger,
while you are full-bodied,
who, I wonder, shall carry across time,
and in his heart, your lovely visage,
and shall be your singer? Who,
other than me, you homeland?

II. The Last Line of an Ode

They climbed the stairs . . .
I could hear suspicious footsteps,
and see beneath their overcoats,
the address of the house and the muzzle of the gun.
They climbed the stairs . . .
And whispered.

The second man among them comes forward,
bends his index finger and knocks . . . knocks on my door!

Damn you . . .
You have shattered the silence!
Damn you . . .
You have driven away the vision
of that very last house.

III. Bats
Bats at my windowsill
swallow up my voice,
and bats at the entrance to my house,
and the bats behind sheets of paper . . .
. . . in some corners,
follow my footsteps closely,
and every turn I take.
Bats on the chair . . .
in the street behind me,
and on the cover of books and the legs of young girls,
wherever my glances take me!

Bats on my neighbor's balcony,
bats that are some kind of device . . . hidden in a wall,
bats about to commit suicide.

I dig a path to the light of day.

Tawfiq Zayyad

Some Words about the Aggression

My country! Yesterday we were not floating on shallows,
and so today we will not drown in shallows!

From here they passed to the east, black clouds,
trampling flowers, children, wheat fields and drops of dew,
and hatching enmities, rancor, graves, and knives.
From here they shall return, though a long time may ensue.

This is how he died, with no notice of his death upon the sand,
a martyr,
a bullet in his head, a scream of oppression and threat.
The killer engraved a new number
upon the barrel of his gun,
then, wolf-like, went looking for a new number.
A few meters away, a newborn child began to cry,
when upon his dark forehead,
there passed an iron chain.

Tell me not: We have won!
This victory is worse than defeat.
We do not regard the surface alone, but instead,
we witness the depth of the crime.
Tell me not: We have won!
We know well that slyness,
and know well that snake charmer
who gives the signal!
It is your master,

breathing his last,
and we shall drag him by the nose,
into a contemptible grave.

What have you stored for the morrow,
you who shed my blood,
robbed my eyes of light,
crucified my pen,
and violated the rights of a peaceful nation
that committed no crime? . . .
What have you stored for the morrow,
you who insulted my flag,
and opened wounds inside wounds,
and stabbed my dreams:
What have you stored for the morrow
But the morrow has not been conquered!

For twenty years you have lived
a summer's dream of pleasing appearance,
and hunted, upon orders from others,
in a sea of tears and blood.
You build for the present day,
but I build high my future.
We are deeper than the sea,
loftier than the lanterns of heaven.
Within us is a vitality of spirit
longer than that expanse that stretches,
in the heart of the infinite.

Which mother was it, I wonder,
who bequeathed you

half the Canal?
Which mother bequeathed you Jordan's bank,
Sinai, and its mountains?
He who robs another's right in war:
how will he protect himself
when the balance swings back?

Then . . . then what? I don't know,
all I know is that the earth is great with child,
and so too the years.
All I know is that justice never fades,
nor is it ever usurped by conquerors.
On this land of mine,
no conqueror ever lasted.
Lift your hands from my people,
and do not feed the fire with twigs.
How can you live on a ship
and fight an ocean on fire?

Lift your hands from my people,
You who are deaf and stuff your ears
with cotton and wax.
For the thousandth time we tell you:
We are not cannibals, we do not cut children's throats,
nor kill peaceful people.
We do not plunder houses
or the harvests of some field.
We do not blind eyes
or steal antiquities.
We do not know how crime tastes,
we do not burn books or break pens,

or bully the weak.
Lift your hands from my people,
You who are deaf and stuff your ears
with cotton and wax.
For the thousandth time we tell you:
We swear by the light
that shines upon this free soil:
We shall not lose an atom of it!
We shall never bend, beneath fire and steel,
not a hair's breadth!

A mere stumble this,
and often does a man of high purpose stumble.
It was one step back,
for the sake of ten steps forward!

Short Poems

Snow on Occupied Lands

What can kill resolve
in a nation engaged in struggle?
My homeland, however much they choose to forget,
has witnessed the coming of a thousand conquerors
who then dissolved,
just
like
snow!

Proverbs

Our ancestors used to quote a proverb:
"A jackal who swallowed a scythe"!

Whatever the wind brings
will be blown away by storms,
and he who plunders another
will live his life
in fear!

A Passing Matter

I am no soothsayer,
and have no divining rod.
I am no astrologer,
but this I do know:
Injustice
is a passing matter
that does not last!

The Mulberry Bush

When in the morning they passed by it,
the mulberry bush whispered to them:
"Go play with fire as long as you like,
but no
rightful claim
ever dies!"

The Last Time

When they trampled upon it,
a flower by a water spring called out:
"You occupier, know your limits!
This is the last time!
This is
the last time!"

A Mirage

Surround, surround,
and blow up
all those we love.
Burn my house, burn my harvest, and burn every book,
but the mirage of a stream can never quench thirst.

Patience! That fang will never conquer my child's smile.
Patience, mother, patience, sister, be patient and endure,
for we shall nail these hands above the doors,
and with these fangs shall slaughter the beast,
and the nightingale shall sing,
and build its nest upon our doorstep,
and a dawn for our nation shall come,
and only those we love shall make it break.

An Incident at Night

He opened our door, suddenly,
and collapsed, like a wall,
with terror in his eyes.
On his forehead were two pomegranate blossoms,
and on his left shoulder,
his cotton robe was kneaded with his left shoulder.
. . .
He said nothing.
We sprang towards him,
and the silence was shattered by a woman:
"Where have you been?" she screamed, "the father of my
young children?"

He did not reply,
But from his pocket he pulled out
an embroidered handkerchief,
one we all recognized.
It was bloodied and torn.
The woman screamed: "O God!"
Then fell to pieces.

"Lord, how many deaths must we escape these days"
groaned the man collapsed like a wall on the ground.
He grits his teeth, like one who has swallowed
a fiery knife:
"I was walking behind him when I heard the gun,
the machine gun.
I was walking behi . . .
It was a moonlit night, the river like a mirror,
and we were crossing the bridge, barefoot and in silence,
like a band of wary thieves.
It was a moonlit night, and there were ten of
us . . . twenty . . . fifty
I can't remember how many.
Back homewards we were heading,
back to you, you land of torment,
and mud houses . . .
and scent of our families . . .
you handful of grass and soil.
We were coming back like a band of thieves,
crossing the bridge barefoot and silent,
when they suddenly sprang upon us, like wolves,
and opened up with their machine guns . . .
barely two meters separated us . . .
O God, how many deaths must we

escape from these days!
We carried not even a dagger,
and we fell upon each other,
we fell like a swarm of flies."
What about him? We cried,
uncertain and apprehensive?
And him?
Silence.
Sobbing.
Knives of torment.
. . .
"They gathered us all in two ditches,
and threw in some earth.
I was not dead, and when they left,
I rose . . . the river was like a mirror,
and it was a reddish night, drowned in mist.
I crawled, silent, terrified and in torment,
and there before me lay his handkerchief.
I recognized it and picked it up."
. . .
In a corner of that room sat a pregnant woman crying,
and a boy and a girl.
You, with bloodshot eyes . . . what use is crying
when blood itself these days
is worthless?

You scent of a family,
And you, house of mud,
And you, handful of grass and soil:
How much death must we swallow for your sake!
And how many kinds of torment!

Bury Your Dead and Rise

. . . We had to drink it,
even the glass,
that twisted cup of bitterness.

We needed to be slaughtered,
like lambs,
for the clock of history has gone mad.

We needed to flee,
like a flock of chickens,
and to feel disgrace in our bone.

Never mind! Our flesh is a body
floating upon a bitter sea,
towards banks that never betrayed us,
nor ever we betrayed.

O soil, all golden,
ruby and ivory,
our love is stronger than love, and richer.

So, bury your dead and stand up straight,
and if tomorrow has flown away,
it shall not escape us.

We are not lost . . . But . . .
Cast and molded anew.

Fawzi al-Asmar[15]

Something New

A new day must dawn,
a day
when the sun is afraid of slaves,
a dawn that scoffs at chains,
and iron,
and the child shall take up the chant,
and trample underfoot an envious serpent,
and strike the very heart of the land,
breaching dams.
The child in our souls is something new.

At our cvcry dawn . . . a new day,
and upon our shoulders is iron.
We shall remove that crucifix,
that burden readied for us.
We shall remove it,
to hug our nation's new dawn.

What is a human being worth . . . in darkness
or in an ancient tune?

---

15 Fawzi al-Asmar is a young critic and journalist whose family originated from Jaffa. He currently works for the newspaper *Haolam Hazeh* (*This World*). He was dismissed several times from his job and pursued by the Israelis. He could be considered the most prolific writer in occupied Palestine, and closely follows developments in its literary and cultural spheres. He has published several literary and nationalist works and was arrested in late 1963 after he published two books: *Muhammad and Christ* by Khalid Muhammad Khalid and *A Tear and a Smile* by Jibran Khalil Jibran.

In the darkness of his tomb
his light is deepest darkness,
with the visage of an owl,
its song like a dirge;
What is a human being worth
if he abandons the raging fire?
Nothing can be called new
once abandoned.

What is love worth when muffled in bliss?
At the dawn of a day,
cloudy, jaded, infertile,
love has grown tired of clouds,
and hugs the new dawn.
The love in our souls is something new.

The Ancient Temple

In my ancient temple, I have not ceased
to gather words together,
and melt them in a flaming forge,
and mold them into a tune,
for a song of solace and hope.
Its melody will come
from our fire's melody and our great love,
from the light that shines in our hearts,
from our wounds,
wounds that lend color to saffron,
from the strong arms of that swarthy man
who smashes rocks,
from our bereaved land,
from the tears of springtime upon flowers.

In that ancient temple,
the wicks of our candles are melting, in weariness,
their smoke overflowing, in anger,
to caress the wall!
And the darkness leaves a smudge of our shame
on the brow of its ancient ceiling.

That ancient temple is still replete
with our incense.
We burn incense each day,
an offering to God,
to the spirit of our ancient Lord!
We slaughter sheep,
and at each dawn we slaughter sheep
and melt down their grease on that ancient altar,
an offering to God,
to the spirit of our ancient Lord!
Smoke overflows,
all bunched together in that circle of fog,
colorless,
odorless,
as though our fire were ashes,
and our ram sacrificed in vain!

In that ancient temple
our voices still repeat that hymn,
alongside thousands upon thousands
of the lost and wandering,
raising them to our ancient God,
for Him to accept our hymn
and our fire,

and our fattened ram,
and accept our incense,
an offering from an ancient temple!

This Be the Road

`Uqba ibn Nafi`, conqueror of the Maghrib, said when he stood before the ocean: "I swear to God, if the *Jihad* ordered me to plunge into this ocean on horseback, I would do so."

Mighty were our fortresses,
charged with rancor, and boiling in our cauldrons,
and a rose-like heroism
redolent with fragrance
in our luxuriant woods.
Our caravans set forth
to win glory, and their thirst was quenched
from jars filled from our springs,
caravans that relate, from that bloodied land
of honor and pride,
stories exhaling fragrance upon our homes.
To victory! O land of glory!
The heart of glory lies in our homes.
To victory! O land of God!
The spirit of God is in our blood!
God is in our blood,
and rancor too,
till the horizons reveal a sun,
hugged by our flaming torches.
We are Tariq's descendants,
or else of those who went with Tariq,
conquering across the Maghrib,

each saying: I am the Arab youth,
revolution and uprising are in my blood.
They brought down from the sky
bitter poison upon Roderic,
from flashing Arabian swords,
and our coasts burnt their ships.
We inherited war,
and resignation was never a trait of ours.
We inherited the cry of God,
still echoing on our coasts.
"I swear to God,
if the Jihad orders me to plunge into this ocean"
our bombs[16] would be unleashed,
and rancor,
till the horizons reveal a sun,
hugged by our flaming torches.

16 The word *qanabil* (Arabic: bombs) can also refer to a herd of fifty horses.

Nazih Khayr[17]

Illusion

In their hearts are farms of mist,
and in their eyes is the habit of fire.
They extended a hand of destiny,
to a world without destiny,
and the journey of that current is a story
that passes through their souls,
and comes back,
through routes of misery,
emptied . . .
of all morning hopes,
emptied of their genuine dawn,
and illusion is still their eternity, and still,
in their hearts are farms of mist,
and in their eyes is the habit of fire!

Forgotten by Christmas

It was Christmas . . . and it passed without a story,
telling how people come together on feast days.
Not a single hug . . . not one fragrant whisper
was content to dance with a Christmas candle.
For Christmas I had cultivated
a bunch of narcissus, and Christmas passed,
and my sorrowing narcissus was swaying.

---

17 Nazih Khayr is a young poet with a distinctive and powerful poetic style, but his poems are short, and their import is not yet entirely clear. However, he is a poet of promise in occupied Palestine.

Do not sorrow . . . for tomorrow,
the dew will be your companion,
in some rising ground, eager
for a date.
Tomorrow—alas for tomorrow!—when at break of dawn,
about Talal and his robe will be my song.
On the eve of some moonlit morning,
large of eye, and streaked with kohl
by a soft and dewy breeze,
don't be sad . . . what they said will not tire you:
"That poor wretch . . . Forgotten by Christmas!"

Rashid Hussein[18]

Noble horses

In other countries,
a child is born small,
and upon his days they pour warmth and light,
and tell him some lines
from the story of the sun.
And behold! That child who was small,
has become a man . . . a tall and large human!

In our villages, a child is born a prince,
and upon his eyes they pour night and pious vows,
and on his soft skin they build palaces.
And behold! The child who was once a prince
has become a dwarf . . . a small man,
a mud drinker, ruminating husks.

In other countries, a child grows older,
and with him grow all life's meanings,
and on his forehead grow stars and hopes.
In our villages, amidst billows of smoke,
a child will grow, as do the congratulations,
and they will say:
Your sweet boy is now the dream of pretty girls,
A groom of marriageable age,
the son of so and so.

---

18 Rashid Hussein Mahmoud was born in the village of Masmas, a village of the Northern Triangle, in 1936. He completed his elementary education in Umm al-Fahm and now works in journalism.

And now a generation of grooms invades my country,
a generation of boys, grown older,
like noble horses,
their minds filled with phantoms
of gray thought.
and their hopes come to rest with "Su'ad"
at the feet of "Su'ad,"
at some henna on the palm of "Su'ad"!

If only my people could give birth to a child,
just as a child,
and not throw mud on his eyes,
and perhaps might bloom, on my country's land,
a new generation of knights . . . in my country.

Children give birth to small children
who then become men . . . who suffuse the night with fire,
and perhaps I may glimpse,
around me,
eagles,
not birds aping eagles!

In other countries,
It is the end that worries people,
but in our villages, it is the beginning.
All they care about is that a wife
will give birth to a male child,
so they can say:
That woman comes from a proud and noble lineage.
She delivered a male child,
his face like the moon.

And they will say: her husband is a mighty stallion,
A real man . . .
Or an Arabian steed, an undefeated hero
Only for their son to sit and swat flies,
An earthworm in a land . . .
made of dust!
Let him be dumb . . . blind . . . an owl in a ruin,
and let his father die, and his mother too,
and let his midwife die of joy,
yet he is a male,
with a face like the moon.
His mother is the daughter of a noble man,
a mare she is, who does not stumble,
and her husband is a real stallion . . . a victorious conqueror!

My homeland! Tell me, my homeland, when
will you suffuse us, just once, with light instead of slumber.
You have drowned us in honey and in milk.
Then might slave markets be destroyed,
and black and noble horses plunge into the fire,
and perhaps the flight of birds turns round,
and see! They've become hawks and eagles!

Thoughts and Echoes

The sky wept, to console him,
but the weary man grew wearier.
Does a man, drowning in the sea,
ask the sky above for a deluge?
Does he long for the rain that freezes his body
and aggravates his toil?
No, you sky! Stop!

That wretched sorrowing man is shattered!
Walk on, brother, and do not despair.
To mock your calamities is more rewarding.
On the pages of history we shall inscribe
one line of glory above another.
Walk on, and renew that resolute hope,
and be not a slave to despair!

Mahmoud Dasuqi[19]

The Prison and the Struggle

Prison shall not scare our free men, when jailed
or tortured, somewhere in this land, or detained.
Prison shall not scare lions that roar,
and fear no exile and torture, whatever they do to them.
Prison shall not scare one robbed of property,
his house a ruin, its traces effaced.
He is a wanderer, without land or country,
house, wealth, or work.
Where is this "justice" you boast about?
Does "justice" mean "permits" and "detention camps"?
Does "justice" mean "concentration" and "confiscation"
and "present absentee," where a man is ridiculed?
Rise against injustice and despotism and unite!
Till when will our people bear injustice?
March forward, and let us destroy chains, now rusted,
tearing down injustice, fearless and daring.
Years of darkness passed through our homeland,
but our ancestors never suffered an ordeal like ours.
"David!" You thought prison would scare us,
But we shall fear neither prison nor torture . . . so go
ahead! Detain us!

---

19 Mahmoud Dasuqi is from the village of al-Tayybeh. His poetry, classical in style, closely follows Arab events. He published a poetry collection entitled *Alongside Free Men* in 1959. He followed this up with another called *The Pageant of Free Men*, which was confiscated by Israel and its sale prohibited. It is thought that he published a play called *The Court of Al-Mahdawi*, and a collection of short stories called *The Horrifying Massacre*.

Here we shall revolt against an injustice that surrounds us,
and today our people are like a raging volcano.

A People and Tents

My country, does it suffice us to kiss your soil,
and these stones, after this absence?
My country, are we to remain tent inhabitants?
To remain acquainted with bitterness of torment?
Will wretchedness remain our ally,
from cradle to youth?
Are our hopes to remain distant,
and will our distant dreams remain like a mirage?
Are we to remain inhabitants of these tents,
or inside caves, or atop some hills,
when a land, a home, and an olive tree,
call out, wailing over their owners,
longing for its displaced people,
and drenching the earth with tears?
My country, know that in my blood is a revolt,
and that I shall return, no matter the obstacles.
I shall return, despite these frontiers, to my home,
after a long absence.
I shall return, so sing, you birds,
and bring to people the glad news of my homecoming.

Short Story

Abu Salam

At Last, the Almond Tree Is in Bloom[20]

"In my romantic youth I read the Charles Dickens novel *A Tale of Two Cities* and hero-worshipped Sydney Carton, who sacrificed his life to save the husband of the woman he loved when he exchanged with him his clothes and place in the Bastille, and beneath the very shadow of the guillotine.

"Like other people, none of my heroes survived decay. They came and went, as my years came and went, to the point where only one hero survived, Hugo's philosopher, Gringoire, that wretched vagabond in *The Hunchback of Notre Dame*. When asked to substitute himself in the same way in order to save the pretty gypsy Esmeralda, he refused. Asked what makes him so attached to life he responds: 'My greatest happiness is spending all my days, from morning till evening, with a man of genius, myself, and this is a very beautiful thing.'"

"What about Arabism?"

"Would you please refrain from censure and sarcasm at this, our very first interview, and after my twenty-year absence from you?"

This is precisely what I intended when I reminded Mr. M. of Arabism. He had paid me a surprise visit at night, which astonished me and raised my suspicions, and he had begged me to listen patiently to him.

---

20 This is the second segment of a work in six chapters entitled *The Sextet of Six Days*, which can stand by itself as a short story. It was published in *Al-Jadid* in May 1968.

We had been very close friends in primary and secondary school. Together, we had founded the very first secret society at our primary school to fight the British, a society that only included its two founders, having no consequence except addiction to cigarettes, which we regarded as something required by secret activities. We wore dark glasses to hide the tears of men and when we celebrated the end of our secondary school years, we said our goodbyes and made promises to one another.

Thereafter, our paths had diverged. M. had traveled to Jerusalem to join the Government Arab College to finish his studies, then returned to our town, where he worked as a teacher of English at its secondary school, a job he still held.

But after the creation of Israel, our ties had been totally severed. He had even avoided saying "hello" when we met by accident on a street. At first, this rupture had pained me, but then I got used to it and dropped him from my life, realizing he was the sort of person who resembled a woman who, while unmarried, would hardly finish one story before reading the next, but once married, would abstain from reading anything—not even the strips of newspapers in the toilet.

This friend of mine, with whom I used to celebrate the conquests of Khalid ibn al-Walid, the elegies of al-Mutanabbi, and the freethinking reflections of Abu'l `Ala', as well as Arabism, this friend had married his job. So how could he retain his job in Israel when the authorities mandated severance of all ties with friends or relatives considered troublemakers by these authorities, even if that person was your full brother, son of your father and mother?

Then he had suddenly knocked on my door, one night following the Six-Day War, sat facing me after a twenty-year rupture, and said: "Please listen to the very end."

What had made a lion enter into his heart, so that he dared to visit me?

Mr. M. then continued his tale: "Sydney Carton dropped from my album of heroes like the hairs I first shaved off my face. However, Dickens's title, *A Tale of Two Cities*, kept haunting and mystifying me, affecting my taste throughout these long years. Its effect appeared in ways that puzzled me at first, but then I surrendered. Indeed, I would carry it around with me affectionately, respectfully, like a man wearing an amulet that his mother had tied around his neck since his birth.

"In my early days of being so strangely affected, I began writing *A Tale of Two Cities* of my own, two cities in our homeland, Haifa and Nazareth, and wrote its first chapter, but the story ended right there, so I dropped it. I then decided to specialize in two fields, English and the law, but did not do so. I experimented with writing verse in both English and Arabic and merely experimented with hot air, in both languages. It pains me that I begat only one child, being intensely desirous of two. You should ask your own son, a pupil of mine in secondary school, and he will tell you that I assign for reading only two books, two poets to learn by heart, two men of letters to compare, and two hours for the exam. Other things in my life, which I need not mention, confirm the dominance of this dualism, through that magical title, *A Tale of Two Cities*, over my taste and mind. But surely you must have noticed this when we were intimate friends in our youth. Have you forgotten that you guys used to call me 'Father of Two Chins'?"

"You were heavyset built, with puffed cheeks."

"No, but like all of you, I only had one chin. This nickname stuck, however, because I liked repeating the sentence: 'I care not if a chin is well combed or streaked with kohl,' i.e., two chins, a man's and a woman's, two, *A Tale of Two Cities*. This is the duality, the amulet I carried around my neck since childhood."

(This old friend of mine is elegant in both dress and speech. He talks at length but without affectation. I let him speak at length as I used to do in the past, particularly since his surprising visit astonished me and I was curious to know what he was after. I think I have begun to grasp his purpose and say to myself: It must be one of two things. Either his conscience began acting up because of this war and so, after twenty years, he's come to justify that rupture by telling me about that duality, or else someone must have sent him to me on some errand, and he wants to restore my friendship by talking about that magical duality. So, I keep a careful distance and long for him to come to an end.)

He said:

"This is why my astonishment did not last long as the car carried us upwards, for the first time after that war, on the winding road of Tal'at al-Laban, on the way from Nablus to Ramallah.

"A loud sigh escaped my lips when we passed the first bend, and my tongue trembled, as did the steering wheel. To my colleagues who were with me in the car I cried out: I have been dreaming of this winding road for the last twenty years. This ascent has never been absent from my memory, not for a single day. I remember every single bend on this road. There are four of them: count them. These mountain peaks guard the green valley below. There are ten of them: count them. And this pure air whose fragrance I know: I have been breathing its scent all my life. This place is mine!"

(Fine, I now understand why this poor fellow has come after a twenty-year rupture. O friend of my youth: how hard has fate treated us! Forgive my doubts. I am about to get up and hug him, but he gives me no time to do so.)

Mr. M. continued:

"Upon my insistence, my colleagues consented that I stop the car at the last bend, the fourth. They descended to join me to breathe the air and fill our eyes with the sight of the mountains and that protected plain. Almond trees filled both plain and mountains. Shouldn't they have called them the Almond Bends? Some inner impulse made me want to prostrate myself and something in my eyes was dissolving in tears . . . I felt like one who had just witnessed a miracle, or as if I was reliving my years of youth in the playing fields of youth, which I not only could see but also could experience once more, breathe its air and feel the hot blood of youth, along with the smell of clay ovens and dried figs, and all of this pulsing in my veins.

"But my colleagues would not allow me to tarry. They soon made me drop from the heights of my road bends down to the depths of reality. One of them wanted to continue his journey at once, since our permits did not allow us to make a stop at Tal'at al-Laban, and another colleague made fun of my memory of these road bends, claiming that one day some twenty years ago, I had peed at one road bend. Other comments of the same kind followed, which we teachers are used to making when far from earshot of our students or wives.

"Throughout that trip to Ramallah, Jerusalem, and Bethlehem, and back, I was obsessed by that marvelous event and begged my memory to bring back what had occurred in my youth along that ascent that made me stop at it, like one mesmerized, never wanting to leave it.

"But in vain. When coming back via that road, we descended it without stopping and a colleague saw that I was troubled. He placed his hand on my shoulder to comfort me and said: 'It looks like that ascent called al-`Abhariyya, between Nazareth and Haifa, so you may have confused the two ascents.' He thus managed to lift a heavy load off my chest.

"For the past twenty years, I have been traveling to Haifa twice a week where I teach additional classes in one of its secondary schools and pass by al-`Abhariyya there and back. My colleague convinced me with this simple explanation, although I knew the two ascents were not in the least similar, since I know the secrets of my heart and my weakness for the *Tale of Two Cities*. No doubt the al-`Abhariyya must have been linked to Tal`at al Laban in my imagination. I accepted that explanation and removed a heavy weight from my chest."

(Alas for man! Does he kill in his memory the memories he cannot bear? I used to think that those who had no conscience had hearts of stone and so do not feel its pricking, but the matter was otherwise. It turned out that that man was too weak to kill his conscience, so he kills his memories! So why then does he come to me with this tale?)

My old friend said: "Remember that I have many acquaintances and friends in the West Bank, from school days and beyond: teachers, lawyers, physicians, businessmen, politicians, ministers, and would-be ministers. I visited them all, and we rebuilt, once again, the memories and friendships that had been severed. These people were once more what they had been twenty years before, a dear part of my life. Not a week passes without me visiting them or being visited by one of them. I had previously imagined that they had forgotten me or were ashamed of me, and that they had cut me off from that branch of their tree of life, just as a dead branch is pruned for the tree to grow and blossom."

"But we are a branch that life has caused to blossom."

"You are right. At first, I approached these people hesitantly, not sure how they would receive me, but unexpectedly found in them a longing for old friendships, and indeed pride in them. I found out that they had been following our news and picking them up from the beaks of birds. I also discovered that they estimated us above our own estimation of ourselves. I had wanted to hide from them the fact that I had lived in seclusion for the last twenty years and found out that they knew about this and strongly approved, regarding me in a manner other than how I regarded myself. They raised my esteem, so my self-esteem grew. They lifted me up, so I grew taller, and my head was now higher than the reach of any punch. This is why I told you that they once again became a dear part of my life, the sort of life you knew twenty years ago."

"So, did you visit me openly tonight, with your tall stature?"

"Can I visit in any other way than openly?"

"So, have you visited me for this reason?"

"No, but for a reason that troubles me and keeps me awake at night. I have already told you that my amazement did not last long after Tal`at al-Laban and its road bends had stirred me up so much. I attributed my feelings to that amulet which had been with me since birth, my duality of thought and logic, and my continued exposure to another ascent, the al-`Abhariyya.

"Since that time, I have ascended and descended the road bends of Tal`at al-Laban tens of times. Each time I experienced the onset of that strange and sorrowful longing for it, I would immediately explain it away and relieve my conscience.

"This lasted until that day last February, when I returned with my wife and child from a visit to friends of ours in Old Jerusalem. It was noon when we began to descend the road bends of al-Laban, and the almond trees had begun to blossom, their white and red colors hugging each other in a springtime trance where all ten mountains danced."

"In which language did you compose that poem?

"In the language of my eyes and heart. And you shall hear me to the very end.

"My wife kept insisting that I stop the car so she could gather some almond branches in bloom to decorate our house, but I only agreed to stop at the very last bend, the lowest, where stood an ancient almond tree I think was also there in my past.

"We left the car and cut four branches, which we smiled at, and they smiled back at us.

"When my wife asked me if an almond branch, planted in the soil, would grow to be a tree, I became depressed and started to remember. Do you remember a friend of ours in our early days of youth who fell in love with a girl from Jerusalem or Bethlehem, and how we loved his love?"

"We all fell in love, and we loved his love."

"In fact, our friend's love was more beautiful than ours. He had a story. We were on a trip and alighted right in front of that tree where the Tal`at al-Laban begins. There was a house nearby, with chicken and cows. The house still stands but I can't see any chicken or cows now. We asked the inhabitants for some water and, lo and behold, there were some girls on a trip from Jerusalem cutting off branches of the blossoming almond tree. Among them was our friend's great love. The two met and she handed him a blossoming branch, and the girls disappeared. Were you with us on that trip?"

"Then what?"

"I remember a lovely story about him and can't remember how it reached me. His girlfriend cut off two branches and handed one to him, keeping the other branch. They vowed to keep these branches and to meet the following spring when the almond trees were in blossom. His family would then visit hers and they would ask for her hand in marriage. How did their lovely story end?"

"Why are you so concerned about them?

"I don't know, but I guess some strong impulse drives me to reopen the pages of old friendships, all of them. It is as though I want to tie my present firmly to my past where these ties would never be severed again. That past was bursting with hopefulness, hugging the whole world. It was a pure and open past, like the eyes of a child. It is as though today I want to cling to the strings of that past to rescue myself from this present. Do you think I am just a man drowning and clinging to mere illusions?"

"What happened next?"

"Since the June War I have been wandering like some grieving lover, looking for old friends. Every time I meet one of them, I'm keener to meet the next. Ever since I remembered the story of that friend, I've been looking for him, but none of my friends remembers his story. This intense desire to find him has created a real problem for me. I hardly meet an old friend without asking him how he met his wife! No friend from our days of youth remains unasked except you. This is why I've come to you, so would you please answer the question and relieve me?"

"My friend, you have always been odd, but tonight you are odder than ever. Why this passionate desire to learn something so trivial?"

"Trivial, you say!? I now realize that I only cowered in my shell and my back became bent when I cut my ties with the past. And what indeed is this past? The past is not a certain time period. The past is you and so-and-so, and all my friends. Together, we drew a portrait of that past, and each colored it differently until it assumed its youthful portrait, burning bright and hugging the world and all upon it. I will not reconnect with that past unless the portrait is fully restored with all its colors. That friend of ours, with his beautiful love, I see as the smile on the mouth of that portrait. What past can remain without him? What remains of the Mona Lisa if we wipe away her smile? His story's joyful end will be the meeting of the lovers and their return to one another, while its sorrowful end would be their final parting: this I regard as the truest and most complete end of the springtime of our past, which I'd like to come back as, each year, spring succeeds winter."

"I see you reverting to the tale of two cities, the two branches, the lover and his beloved, the happy ending and the sad ending. But life does not consist in divergent lines but rather in intertwined lines. Why is it not possible that your imagination, reawakened by a springtime longing for towering mountains, made you invent that story?"

"Yes, indeed, my imagination has been awakened and I don't want it to sleep any longer. This is why I'm looking for this friend of mine. Do I gather that you do not remember him?"

"Let me see. If I remember him, I'll let you know."

Mr. M. then left, more troubled than I'd ever seen him. I too sat there, more troubled than I'd ever been in my life. For a few minutes after he left, I had to restrain myself by force from following him to awaken his memory from its sleep of death. But would I be able to awaken the dead?

How could I possibly forget that charming love story whose hero Mr. M. is so keen to remember? How many times have I asked myself: How can a human being kill such love in his heart?

Following the June War, when I had visited that noble and loyal lady in Jerusalem or Bethlehem ("over there," as Mr. M. put it), she had shown me that dry almond branch, which she still keeps, and which almost burst in red and white blooms when she recalled its story, adding that he had visited her along with several of his teacher colleagues, and was throughout very talkative and happy. She had then led them in to see her library and examine her collection of books and works of art. He had noticed the dry almond branch and asked her about it, and she had told him that the almond tree blossoms in February, but he had changed the subject and started telling her about apricots and the very short apricot season. I was utterly taken aback.

However, now that Mr. M. had visited me and told me everything, I finally understood.

I am sure that Mr. M. is truthful in what he forgot and genuine in his longing to remember. Through some strange inner will, he really forgot that he himself was the protagonist of that charming love story and the smile that lit up our days of youth. Should I remind him and so relieve him, as he asked me to? And why should I relieve him? And would I truly relieve him?

If he's grown taller in stature, as he told me, he will be tall enough to get that story and read it. But will he then remember, re-establish the ties with his past and so pull himself out of his present?

At last, the almond tree is in bloom. The two of them had met. Springtime was laughing and fate was giggling.

Drama

Tawfiq Fayyad

House of Madness (A two-act play)

Prelude [by Ghassan Kanafani]

This play, which from beginning to end features a single hero, Sami, a former teacher of history and literature, will appear at first glance to have nothing to do with Arab resistance in occupied Palestine, but a closer examination of the symbols in this play will reveal that impression to be mistaken, since it is now widely recognized that symbolism is the most appropriate form of expression when works of art are produced under the shadow of repression and occupation.

Nevertheless, a few observations need to be made, which may lead to a better understanding of this play:

First, many Arab teachers in the occupied territories have been imprisoned, exiled or fired from their jobs as a result of their teaching. The playwright might himself have been one of these, a fact that helps to explain certain attitudes of the hero of the play.

Second, Arab intellectuals in the occupied territories have been targeted by Israeli intellectuals to tempt them into joining them to formulate certain "common values." It later transpired that this was simply a political ploy to try to defuse Arab unrest, a maneuver soon exposed, which caused them deep bitterness. This constitutes one backdrop to what Sami represents, especially when he talks about Lubna.

Third, presumably, Sami stands on a stage set up in occupied Palestine, and therefore the audience that Sami addresses at certain points in the play is another main character in the action. So he is addressing an audience of Jewish settlers.

Fourth, the play, in addition, constitutes a link in a chain of cultural and political dialogue taking place among Arab intellectuals in occupied Palestine itself. For instance, we note that when Sami speaks, at the start of the play, about "that poet" who assassinated the moon, he is referring to a poem by Mahmoud Darwish, the most prominent poet in occupied Palestine, who wrote a poem entitled "Winter Moon" in which occur the following lines:

> I shall gather together your martyred body,
> dissolve it in salt and sulfur,
> then gulp it down like tea,
> or bad wine, or a poem
> in some lousy festival of poetry,
> and tell the poets:
> O poets of our glorious nation!
> I am he who killed the moon
> whose slaves you are!

Act I: Haifa—Nighttime

In a city quarter by the sea. Only one person appears in the play, Sami, who used to be a teacher of history and literature.

As the curtain is raised, there is a room in total darkness. The darkness persists. Outside are heard the sounds of a strong wind mixed with that of a person snoring.

The snoring stops, but the wind continues to blow. There are occasional sounds of someone raving, and these increase in volume slowly. At the same time, a red light is projected on stage left, which then slowly pans to stage right.

At stage left is a closed door with a key, then a window with an old curtain in the middle of it. A small library with some books. A small wall clock indicating 10 p.m.

The light beam then comes to rest on a desk at extreme right and below the wall clock, to the right of the library. On it is a portrait of a woman, some books, papers scattered without order and containing unpaid bills, an almost empty bottle of wine, and a glass. There is a packet of cigarettes of inferior quality and some cigarettes. At left is a desk lamp, indicating that the owner is an intellectual. At extreme right, and next to the desk, is a closed inner door.

The beam of light finally settles upon the face of a man in the prime of life, long beard, hair disheveled, sitting on an old chair behind the desk, and wearing a tattered winter overcoat over his ordinary clothes. He is seen fast asleep, his head resting on his arms above his desk. The book is open before him.

At the side of his face are many lights, red, yellow, blue, green. These colors are repeated in reverse order until they stop on red.

The sleeper is tormented by the light, as though in a nightmare. The yellow beam is then projected, and at that very moment he utters a loud scream of fear, grabbing his neck with both hands and waking up.

He looks in terror at all corners of the room as his hands slowly drop from his neck. He turns on the lamp with its normal light while still scrutinizing everything around him but avoiding looking at the audience. He turns off the desk lamp as the yellow beam persists in following him wherever he moves, dispensing with the studio lights required by the scene.

Sami (*lighting a cigarette*): A nightmare . . . that terrible nightmare. (*feeling his neck*) Once again! It's as if all the shadows of hell have moved here, to join me in this dilapidated tomb! (*moving his neck*) His savage fingers almost cut through my throat.

(*He turns the light on once more and looks around him in fear. He stops at the book open before him and reads energetically.*)

Rise, rise, Osiris!
I am your son, Horus . . .
I come to restore you to life,
I come to collect your bones,
and reconnect your sinews.
I am Horus, whose father you are.
Horus will give you eyes to see with,
ears to hear with, feet to walk on,
arms to labor with . . .
Here they are, all your body parts whole and sound,
and your body is growing,
and blood is flowing in your veins!
Your own real heart will always be yours,
your past heart!
Rise, rise, Osiris!!
(*He closes the book but continues to repeat even more energetically.*)
Rise, Osiris!
Osiris, rise!

(*He looks longingly at the portrait, then despairs.*)

Lubna! Yes, Lubna! Rather, the dragon!! Who would imagine that such a gentle dove could turn into a terrifying dragon, which plants its horrible paws in my neck?

I was about to go mad! How you torment me, you angel-dragon!? (*in distress*) Hera! That curse has not died!

(*He turns off the desk lamp and stands up, slowly and with difficulty. He stubs the cigarette out in an ashtray, then heads to *the window, as the wind is heard blowing hard. He draws the curtain to the side and looks out, in sadness.*)

Yes . . . There is no moon in the sky! (*He draws back the curtain deliberately, raises one hand up then brings it down nervously as if plucking something.*) That damned poet has brought it down from its heights and raped it in some mad winter night, on a deserted beach. (*He moves his hand expressively.*) Then he dissolves it in salt and sulfur! (*mockingly*) Heh . . . The moon! Yes, the moon in salt and sulfur! (*in wonder*) Indeed, he drank it, like drinking bad wine in some night of pennilessness! (*He moves his hands nervously.*) Why didn't that madman just strangle it? (*He looks in alarm at his intertwined fingers.*) Oh . . . No . . . No . . . (*He lets his hands drop while still contemplating them.*) I would almost lose my mind if I'd seen him do this! To merely imagine him doing so!!! (*He walks toward his desk, still contemplating his fingers, turns the desk lamp on, then turns his hands over and examines them closely.*) I imagined them stained with blood! Damn!

(*He looks in fear at the portrait, turns the light off again, pours out a glass of wine, and stirs the glass with his finger as though dissolving something. He drinks the glass in one gulp . . . then belches, in annoyance.*)

It must be . . . that this madman . . . dissolved the moon in this glass. (*in wonder*) Who knows? He may be one of those implicated in assassinating humans! One of his evil experiments to find something to wipe out the human race . . . more easily than is being done now . . . as agreed upon by world leaders! These leaders are legally entitled to decide if the human race is worthy or unworthy of continued existence!!

But . . . but . . . what has this . . . this so-and-so to do with . . . (*regretfully*) O god of the sky! Even poets have become (*thinking in wonder*) . . . but . . . but (*seriously*).

Moon . . . plus salt . . . plus sulfur . . . plus bad wine. Plus the burning stomach of a madman . . . (*thoughtfully*) equals . . . equals . . . (*belches, in annoyance*) poisonous bubbles . . . (*indicating a movement with his hand*) they rise . . . and rise . . . until they fill the sky with clouds . . . clou . . . (*He listens to the wind, still moving his hand, then continues, nervously.*) and a western, hateful, wind . . . and terrifying phantoms . . . (*He advances to the window, draws the curtain aside, warily, and looks out.*)

It must be that this madman . . . this expert in destroying both the world and himself! No. He must be descended from the jinn! Or else . . . he went mad on his own! He plucked even the stars?! Damn . . . he left nothing in the sky to comfort me. (*He moves to the front of the stage.*) But why was he . . . (*annoyed*) I cannot understand this! Why did he have to choose this particular glass! My glass! So that his evil experiments would have an accursed lab of death!! The height of cheek . . .

(*in wonder*) My glass! And in my house! The height of . . .

(*seriously*) Moon . . . plus sulfur plus . . . the outside world plus . . . a hundred million megatons plus . . . world peace . . . plus . . . (*He pauses and reflects then continues.*) plus . . . world peace . . . equal . . . (*paces back and forth*) equal . . . equal . . . minus humankind . . . minus this terrestrial globe! (*enthusiastically*) And equal . . . of course, equal the Creation . . . less seven days! (*with more enthusiasm*) Naturally, this is the only correct result! (*sitting in triumph at his desk*) Ha! I thought I couldn't solve a human equation . . . (*correcting himself*) A single chemical equation! (*seriously*) No doubt these scientists knew the result beforehand and yet . . . They continue their experiments with it! (*in annoyance*) And at the cost of things that belong to me, at cost to myself! (*He listens to the wind then adds*) The West Wind (*looks at a book on his shelves*). Yes, Shelley! (*sadly*) He too went mad . . . assassinated by the West Wind . . . which threw him into the sea and fed him to the fish! Who could imagine that the fairest of winds would become a murdering criminal! And that lovely face—alas . . . disfigured by a sea crab! That genius—what a loss—becomes fodder for the fire!! And for what? (*sarcastically*) Political justice . . . Yes. Justice! Heh!?

> (*in contempt*) O wild West Wind, thou breath of Autumn's being,
> Thou, from whose unseen presence the leaves dead
> Are driven, like ghosts from an enchanter fleeing.

(*He pours out what's left in the wine bottle and drinks it.*) These poets, they're all mad! It is the wine of hell that their wretched souls pour out until the very last gasp of existence! (*He looks in despair at the bottle then puts it back, repeating in fear.*) And pursued like ghosts! Ghosts!! (*He feels his neck.*) He almost suffocated me, that savage ghost! Lubna's ghost, no doubt! (*angrily*) No . . . no . . . the ghost of that ill-mannered landlord . . . (*He hears the wind clearly, springs up toward the door then sits down again, repeating distractedly and hesitantly.*) At midnight one day, as my boat was in the realm of the dead, and spreading its sails to face its waves . . . (*using hands to express*) the terrifying hands of a cheetah . . . from behind that total darkness, hands that stretched forth . . . then . . . then . . .

with all their madness grabbed my neck! (*in terror*) I almost lost my mind . . . hands stretched straight up to the ceiling! As it grabbed my neck it was turning into a terrifying dragon! Its eyes were burning, its ugly hair turning into sharp scales, biting into every part of my body . . . its savage jaws expanding . . . around my skull (*pointing to his head*) This . . . is the very pit of hell! Its fiery jaws . . . how horrid! I screamed as I fell into that pit, screamed as loud as I could! I was falling . . . falling . . . but did not reach the bottom!! (*in wonder*) But why a cheetah and why a dragon?! (*examining his hands*) Ah . . . no . . . no . . . they are no doubt human hands! It must be that I'm still human . . . Many these days are transformed into apes! Into that species of terrifying reptiles!!

Ahm . . . (*decisively*) No . . . no way can I be transformed into one of these . . . I must remain a human being . . . I must! (*looks again at his hand, smiles and relaxes*) Lubna used to say about them that they were beautiful, like a child's hands!

But . . . (*suddenly falls silent, listens to the wind near the door, then is startled as if by some knocking on the door*) But this savage hand knocking on my door cannot be a human hand! (*Sound of wind again. He springs up at stage front, in anger, his hand pointing sideways to the door.*) What? . . . Is there no law any longer to restrain these bastards? What do they think? That I am their slave!? They can break into my house anytime they want!!! (*He moves a little and fast toward the door.*) No . . . I will not submit to your will, you bastards . . . (*He retreats, finger raised in warning.*) You barbarian criminals! (*listens to the wind blowing, then angrily steps to the door*) It must be that bear . . . the bar owner! No . . . I will not answer your knocking . . . even if you break down the door with your drunken fist. (*Sounds of wind. Moving swiftly to the door.*)

What do you want, you violent fellow? That I should die of thirst for wine? And why? Because I can't afford it? (*petulantly*) I told you. No . . . I won't open . . . break down the door if you can. (*expressing with his hands*) I will strangle you with these two hands . . . (*regards his intertwined fingers in fear*) Ah . . . I owe you nothing . . . Owe you nothing . . . You made your wine from my blood! (*soft wind sounds . . . looks in wonder . . . then relaxes*) To hell with you . . . Yes . . . Perhaps the fat and grease above your heart will suffocate it and stop its pulse. Maybe I'll be rid of you! (*Sits behind his desk, lights a cigarette. Blows out the smoke nervously toward the portrait, then observes the smoke dissipating around him. Looks longingly at the portrait, then picks it up.*) Lubna . . . Where are you, Lubna? You abandoned me to my sorrows. Why? You'd said you'd never leave me. How could you . . .

(*Sound of wind once more. He looks in terror at the window.*) Once more that mad wind. Will it not stop its wailing—for Satan's sake!? It is murdering me little by little!! (*listening*) What's this? . . . Owls hooting outside! No . . . not owls . . . Must be Lubna! Lubna being strangled . . . her death rattle!! (*He taps his finger on the desk.*) Her heart beats!! (*He places his hand on his chest.*) No, my heartbeats . . . Impossible! Impossible that it is her heartbeats!! (*Sound of wind. He springs in terror toward the door.*) Footsteps! Savage footsteps! Tramping . . . tramping . . . these monsters! It must be them . . . these heavy boots!

O God . . . They're coming near, very near! (*retreating madly*) To hell with you, you beggars . . . other doors will open to you but not mine . . . (*He sinks, tired, at his desk.*) Thank God . . . they're leaving . . . going far! Devil take them! . . . (*listening to the gentle wind, absentmindedly*) "Pass gently over western waves, spirit of God." (*in silence, then repeats*) "Your waves are made of dreams, joyful and terrifying, making you terrible and beloved" (*relaxes, expressing with his hand*) gentle and thoughtful . . . (*Sound of strong wind. Suddenly silent then in terror to the door.*) God in heaven! He's coming back!! That heavy boot! Those stomping, threatening steps . . . (*springs up at stage front*) Yes, his steps . . . I know them well! That hunchbacked landlord! He will toss me into the street . . . that tyrant! (*bitterly*) The law is on his side . . . indeed the state and all its authority are on his . . . ready to obey his signal! For his sake it'll even wage war, if he so desires! (*angrily*) As for me . . . I'm a worthless member of the state!! And why?! Because I don't have the same paunch he does! (*finger in warning*) I have nothing left, you raging bull, nothing . . . You've stolen all I own and sold them at auction! And yet you continue to pursue me. I've nothing left except for what you left me: these moth-eaten books! Take them if you like . . . I no longer need them . . . (*heads swiftly to the desk*) And these hateful bills . . . (*he tosses them toward the door.*) Hah . . . what do you think? That you'll enslave me?! No . . . and a thousand times no! You will not succeed . . . you . . . and all the state's apparatus! That rotten apparatus which you run according to your whims! I'll toss you all in hell, all of you . . . do you hear?! I'll never be your slave . . . and will do so alone . . . yes, I still can . . . alone!! (*in contempt*) Is it not enough that you dismissed me from my job and robbed me of everything to starve me to death and make my submission easier!? And why? Because I represent a danger to you and your despicable interests! Because, according to you, I distort history! And distort literature . . . But you don't?!

(*angrily*) What is it you want from me? To teach your children how to become human wolves like you? How to suck blood?! (*listens in wonder, goes swiftly to the window, draws the curtain aside and looks out*) How odd! He's leaving! Disappearing at the end of the lane!! (*relaxes and returns to desk*) Thank God . . . (*turns on the lamp then turns it off, groaning in panic*) He's coming back! Damn . . . That raging bull! (*moves swiftly to window again, looks out warily*) What cheek . . . He's stopped! That bull . . . He examines my window with his evil looks! His eyes burning in the light . . . (*draws curtain back and retreats*) These two eyes . . . can penetrate the thickest wall . . . and darkest windows! These two eyes . . . (*stops angrily*) No one here but me! I . . . I don't know where she is!! I haven't seen her face since that day when . . . (*weakly*) she said she will not let me see her as long as I live! (*comes near the window again, draws the curtain and looks*) My God! . . . He's leaving! Once again disappearing down that lane!! (*returns to stage front*) They're destroying my nerves . . . this hateful war with them . . . almost makes me lose all desire to resist . . . it's paralyzing me . . . slowly paralyzing my spirit. (*firmly*) But I'll never ever surrender!!

(*Looks at audience, surprised. Examines the audience suspiciously as if seeing them for the first time. Approaches them while still examining them.*) God in heaven! You . . . What are you doing here? For Satan's sake, how did you enter my house? How were you able to?!

(*angrily*) What! There is no law anymore in this world!? (*astonished*) Utter cheek! I cannot imagine! How can a person allow himself to enter some house other than his and without the owner's permission?! (*angrily*) Even the zoo . . . even cemeteries have certain visiting hours! Indeed, cemeteries have gates that enclose the dead!! I don't understand how you enter my house as if entering some bar . . . or public toilet!? (*weakly*) Do I owe you anything? (*angrily*) No . . . I will not allow you to sneak into my house, my private life! This is mine . . . mine alone . . . (*furiously*) Why are you looking at me in this way? You'll call me mad . . . Ha!! Isn't it my right to rebel for my freedom? But you'll claim that I'm violating your freedom! To hell with you and your freedom, a freedom you build on the ruins of the freedom of others . . . the ruins of my freedom . . . my ruins!! (*soberly*) You could practice your right to freedom . . . without killing me if you so wished! No one will prevent you!! So why do so at the cost of my freedom? Why must I pay the price out of my freedom? Have I ever robbed you of your freedom? (*firmly*) No, I never did . . . I never even thought of doing so. If you claim that I did . . . this is only to justify your own crimes . . . the crimes you commit against me . . . Simply that . . . (*suspiciously*) I simply can't understand this! Why are you looking at me like this? Damn you . . . What is this farce you are acting out! (*pointing to someone in the audience*) You . . . Why are you looking at me like this? How did you enter my house?! Why!! By what right?

(*angrily*) Why didn't you go somewhere else? To hell for instance . . . Why my house in particular!? (*in astonishment*) O God! . . . Have you seen your eyes? They are burning bright . . . they are . . . It must have been a she-wolf who suckled you! Who knows what demon . . . inhabits that human head!? (*to another person in the audience*) Look at him . . . don't you too think he's . . . as if . . . (*in annoyance*) you too, why are you staring at me? What a horror . . . you're no different from him! (*He looks at one, then the other.*) I can't tell the difference between you! (*He stares at everyone very sharply.*) Damn . . . in the name of Satan, what has happened!! Why do you all assume the same shape when I look at you?! Have you all conspired against me? (*He stares at them suspiciously.*) Impossible that I should look like you in any way! (*firmly*) No, No . . . Impossible! It's frightful that . . . that . . . (*retreating in despair*) Lubna . . . if only you were here . . . you would have tossed these wolves on the street . . . the street . . . But . . . you are far from me now . . . you have gone far . . . you abandoned me . . . you must have done so upon their instructions! They have controlled your small head . . . they enslaved your stupidity!! (*regretfully*) Yes, Lubna . . . (*dreamily*) "Prettiest of eyes are hers . . . prettiest of lilies her breasts . . . tears overflow, throb in the chest, are a prayer in the eyes, our world is still wonderful . . ." (*in despair*) This is how I used to sing to her . . . that is how I sang to her . . . to my beloved Lubna! But she turned a deaf ear to my songs and left me like this, a victim of loneliness . . . tortured by night and ravaged in spirit by day!

(*bitterly*) No, our world is no longer wonderful, but an unbearable hell instead . . . (*annoyed*) the West Wind . . . the phantoms . . . the tramping of savage boots at midnight . . . the freedom of human wolves!! (*sadly*) Her shade . . . her phantom . . . that which my soul flies after whenever it passes . . . like a moth to a fire! (*as if seeing a shade*) "My love, where are you heading? Your faithful lover is coming, the lover who sang to you the prettiest of tunes . . ." (*weeping at the door like one who misses her*) Lubna . . . Lubna . . . (*in despair, returns to his desk*) Her shade once more! How tormented am I at losing her! (*He sits in weariness at his desk, listens to the softly blowing wind, then hums dreamily.*) You're with me . . . let the winds blow . . . let the thunder peal . . . (*in longing*) Her voice was pretty . . . Lubna . . . (*with regret*) This is how she sang to me whenever we were at the seashore . . . she loved me . . . and I loved her. Her voice was like the singsong of a lost spirit (*listens to the sound of the wind, then repeats*) You're with me . . . let the winds blow . . . and the snows fall . . . (*distracted*) at morning's breezes . . . and when the sun pours its fragrance through my window . . . that compassionate cooing used to reach me from behind her window . . . and in the evening. I used to visit her house in secret to hear her . . . she was always singing . . . my heart was attached to her window . . . and one joyful morning I saw her . . . I saw that green lake! That lake in her eyes that stretched to the far horizon . . . that sun-tanned dawn in her small face . . . silk stretched upon the jasmine of balconies . . . female innocence hovering happily . . . carnation blooming upon her chest!! (*in regret*) Yes, you lake of greenery . . . you flowering garden of passion . . . what tempest has passed over your branches? What dragon has come to settle in your fountain, you braids of amber? Ah, my Lubna . . . my lost Lubna . . . (*weeps*) You're with me . . . Yes. Let the winds blow . . . Let them blow . . . Let the snows fall. Let them fall . . . You're with me . . . Hug me, my darling . . . harder . . . harder . . . your heart is an ever warm hearth to me! . . . to me . . . you're with me. (*in despair*) Where have they gone, all these whisperings as the winds blow? Those mutterings as the waves break at our feet on the seashore! How did you forget them, Lubna? How? It's as if you never uttered them!! (*He picks up the portrait and gazes at it closely.*) Lubna as I knew her (*He replaces the portrait and remembers.*) It was a hard winter night . . . the first shimmer of light in my fate . . . the first spark in the fireplace of my heart! (*standing, in love and longing*) Like a warm smile she appeared from behind the wilderness of my life . . . delicate and sweet . . . I worshipped in the prayer niche of that little goddess, praying in the paths of the forest. (*He kneels in prayer and expressing with his hands.*) "Yes, love of my heart . . . it is but your love that golden light dancing upon those branches . . . and these lazy clouds floating in the sky . . . and that running breeze refreshing my forehead . . ." (*He rises with effort to face the audience.*) Once I knew her this is how I came to pray to her . . . to Astarte . . . little innocent Astarte! Astarte the dove . . . Astarte the mother . . . and when in the early months of her pregnancy. (*smiling happily*) That's lovely . . . Lubna . . . (*pointing out*) Pregnant Lubna! (*laughing*) I am almost going mad . . . that little goddess . . . pregnant . . . a little god that gently seeks my company . . . mine . . . her cheeks reddened when (*shyly*) I started to feel with my hands that wonderful bulge in her body . . . she shyly scolded me . . . like a child, I longed to see that doll, my doll that Lubna was hiding from me . . . she slapped my hand to stop it (*fervently*) so I hugged her . . . and kissed with all my love every part of her body . . . her locks of hair . . . her forehead . . . her long lashes . . . her rosy cheeks . . . her lips . . . and that wonderful roundness . . . that doll hidden so carefully for me! She'd push me away shyly . . . (*kneeling*) and then I knelt at her bare feet, those beautiful feet . . . the feet of little Astarte . . . Astarte the mother . . . feet damp with my tears of happiness (*standing with vigor*) like a shadow, I remained seated by her feet . . . all those months of her pregnancy . . . I never left her side . . . mother of the god . . . I attended to her every comfort . . . I watched that roundness brimming with life . . . and the joy of a young girl . . . day after day! When she fell asleep at my side . . . I would not sleep! I would watch that roundness quietly rising and falling . . . (*laughing*) I used to imagine it growing larger and larger . . . and then . . . as the iris opens its petals, I imagined it opening! From it appears that small face . . . that gentle angel . . . and I'd open the palm of my hand to hug it . . . it would run away . . . and hide! The iris would close its petals, and I would close my eyelids, contemplating her wonderful slumber! (*happily*) I was happy . . . I filled the house with little dolls! (*energetically*) All kinds of dolls! I removed from the clouds all their embroidered dresses, and with their painted fabrics I wove dresses for the dolls! To the dancing flowers I stretched my hand . . . and from their folds I scooped the joyfulness of their colors . . . and embroidered his small cradle! Yes . . . I even prepared his cradle! We must do so . . . grant happiness to our kids . . . grant them a heathy life which they can live out and we pass on to them its torch in the proper manner that they should carry it! (*in despair*) But . . . but not . . . (*looks, astonished, at the wall clock*) O my God! I need to leave! . . . I'm late! (*listens at the window, then relaxes*) The wind is calm . . . (*advances, draws curtain, and looks outside*) The lane is deserted . . . and death has shrouded its windows! (*advances to door, awkwardly rearranging his overcoat*) She must be waiting . . . she always used to wait for me at this hour . . . I must leave! (*opens door, then looks at wall clock*) How this damned clock betrays me! I ought to have destroyed it . . . I must destroy it! My rendezvous with Lubna has come and gone . . . I'm late for my visit to my child! Damned is he who hands his children over to forgetfulness, so let me go now . . . (*He leaves, closing the door behind him.*)

Act II

Curtain rises. Same room and same objects as in Act I. Darkness continues for a little while, as the sound of a strong wind is heard outside.

The red beam of light falls on the wall clock, then on the empty chair before the desk. The light pans slowly right until it settles on the door of the room at stage left, while sounds of muffled coughing are heard outside the door along with the sound of a key turning but as though the door is difficult to open.

He barely opens the door, which creaks, and Sami enters sideways, agitated and hugging his overcoat tightly, still coughing, and with the red light on him till the very end.

(*angrily, as he tries to close the door while coughing*) That mad wind . . . the god of winds must have gone mad! Damn him . . . that wretch . . . damn everything! (*He locks the door from the inside.*) And damn this bloody door! (*making sure it is locked*) Nothing but misery has come to me through it! (*He moves away a little then comes back to make sure it is locked.*) Can't human beings live without doors?! (*coughing*) Isn't it time for these cowards to stop . . . to stop butchering each other?! (*goes to window while straightening his disheveled hair*) What curse was it that murdered the peace of the night, violating its silence with the tramping of its jinni hooves . . . their terrifying neighing! (*He draws the curtain aside and looks out.*) Let death overtake this whole city for ever . . . (*makes sure the window is closed*) The West Wind! That terrible and mighty wind! There is no more sand on the beach! I almost went mad! My eyes saw a terrible sight! How ugly things are! (*draws curtain aside again and looks out*) That beach of death! Not a single crab remains at the bottom of the sea! Ah . . . the horror! Its dark and frightful waves! Like ghosts they were creeping toward me! They would rise and rise then break into foam, whirling savagely around my feet which were slipping fast into the pit! I almost surrendered to their ferocity! I almost plunged into the chasm of their horrible night! (*weakly, redrawing curtain*) With such speed! Ah . . . What misery! Who could have imagined it? (*moving angrily to desk*) Why didn't that savage wind carry off the waters of the sea with it to hell! Or any other place! Why the sand on the beach!? Is there nothing else but sand in this world that you can carry with you?!

(*points to window*) For Satan's sake, why didn't it carry away with it this turgid world . . . perhaps it would later bring a better one . . . or else . . . or else . . . this sinful city!?

(*faces audience angrily*) Or this tomb . . . this house and all its embalmed objects! But it didn't! Just to challenge me . . . with . . . these sands . . . Damn! (*sits at desk wearily, slapping his knees*) It must be one of those bankrupt nights, this night that gave birth to me after hard labor! (*silent, then sarcastically*) Yeah . . . in the toilet! My poor mother . . . she found nowhere to deliver me except in the toilet?! (*in despair*) What misery! Was the world too narrow for her? In the toilet?! (*angrily*) But there is an excuse for her! It's these ferocious warplanes . . . it is they that gave birth to me in the toilet while giving birth to utter madness and hundreds of bombs . . . these bombs they rained down upon the city that night . . . without stopping! These barbaric thunderclaps . . . these terrifying earthquakes . . . it is these that gave birth to me . . . and in the toilet! It was as if I were . . . I were . . . (*standing and facing the audience nervously*) Yes, that night of terror! (*in doubt*) But . . . is this not precisely what bankruptcy amounts to? Bankruptcy of the mind? A world bankrupt of all its moral standards! Indeed, the bankruptcy of all humankind?! (*angrily*) What else can it mean . . . that this hell should precede my birth? That I should be the offspring of fear and terror!? That a mad band of blacksmiths and coppersmiths would relieve the Creator from managing the factory of life . . . for that band to lord it over the world! Isn't this precisely what madness means? Indeed, the very height of madness! That the blacksmith and coppersmith should become responsible for this factory! (*sarcastically*) Heh . . . I . . . heh . . . was made by a blacksmith! No doubt my end will be at his hands! (*bitterly*) What misery . . . I can't even imagine it! But it's the truth . . . and the proof is that I was born in a toilet! (*sarcastically*) War . . . war for the sake of a better life! Heh . . . so that my mother would deliver me in a toilet! And before my term too! Yes . . . yes indeed, so that toilets would become the cradles for the birth of mankind! And why? For me to have a better life! What misery! (*to audience*) Is it . . . is it . . . (*stops suddenly and examines audience with suspicion, pointing in astonishment at audience*) What? You . . . still here? What the devil are you doing here? Ah . . . How stupid! Did you imagine I'd leave this house to you? What nerve! What utter nerve! I almost forgot you're here, almost totally forgot. I shouldn't have. But this must never escape my mind. You occupy my house . . . and rob me of my freedom without any justification and without being deterred by any law. No . . . No . . . ! I will never forget, I promise you . . . Bad luck for you! But I will fulfill my promise! (*sarcastically*) No doubt you find me a bother! Ha . . . (*seriously*) You are right! It's only natural for a criminal to be bothered by the effects of his crime! And only natural that this would drive him to commit another crime . . . indeed, to multiply his crimes . . . so he can finally wipe out all that reminds him of his first crime! This is a law . . . In fact, it is your constitution, your basic law! (*suspiciously*) Why are you looking at me like this? Why do you all assume the same shape when I look at you . . . or address you?! This ugly glowering look . . . this dreadful silence, this savagery that dwells in the corners of your mouths! O God! Even your breathing . . . is heavy and slow! Like the breathing of starving wolves . . . the hissing of snakes parched with thirst for blood! (*seriously*) I am not mistaken . . . it's the truth! But I've rattled on too much, as though I've got nothing left to do. I shouldn't have bothered you with a problem that concerns me alone and bothers me! I don't know! Perhaps it does concern you too? It must concern you also . . . I didn't invite you into my house! But you entered it without my permission! You broke into it violently! (*pointing to a woman in the audience*) Does this problem concern you? I mean . . . I mean that you may be a criminal . . . and wipe out all traces of your crime?!! (*correcting himself*) Oh . . . I didn't mean . . . I meant . . . I meant . . . that your infant might be forged by a blacksmith . . . who then . . . kills him? Yes, that's precisely what I meant.

(*happily*) I thank you . . . I don't need to, but I do thank you! The mere fact that you understand me . . . the mere fact that you agree with my views . . . that you will try to convince others that I'm right . . . means that I shall win in the end . . . my victory! It's only natural that you don't agree . . . your infant must no doubt be a human being!

(*retreating, vigorously*) What mother would agree with such madness . . . that a toilet be her newborn's cradle? No mother in the world would agree! We must all refuse to agree . . . we must stand up for all the mothers of the world!

(*angrily*) But my mother . . . delivered me in the toilet . . . and no one in this world stood up for her! Not one single mother objected! For Satan's sake, what might have happened had she simply received me in the palms of her hands?! What might have happened had that hell swamped the whole world while she . . . while she sat on that toilet seat?! (*contemptuously*) Of course, it's only natural for you to laugh! You think it's a personal matter . . . only natural for you not to deviate from everyone else! The law decrees that you will learn the truth when it's too late! This is your nature! The end of the world . . . How can a mother laugh at such a tragedy! How can a mother not rebel against such an insult to her motherhood?!

(*vigorous, expressive*) What mother would not wish to hug her newborn closer . . . hug it to her heart, kiss its mouth . . . watch it as it suckles at her breast with toothless gums . . . as it tickles her breast with its tiny fingers! The height of happiness . . . Every mother loves this!

(*retreating sadly*) But my mother was not so lucky . . . She never saw me once kissing her breast! In these very moments when she was giving me life . . . she lost her own! (*resentfully*) The hemorrhage. Yes, that bright red hemorrhage . . . that's what killed her, and without my father being able to do anything for her! Anything! (*angrily*) What could he have done amid that hell that was sweeping the world? What?! He didn't know! No one consulted him! In fact, they all conspired against him. (*in great anger*) Yes, they conspired against him . . . the entire world . . . and that bright red hemorrhage will always be the stain left by a horrific crime . . . staining its hands for ever . . . the hands of the entire world! Yes, the entire world . . . is responsible for this agonizing tragedy . . . the tragedy of my birth! The world will forever bear its burden upon its shoulders . . . forever! (*weakly*) Isn't this the very essence of misery, that a human being should suckle at a strange breast . . . that one should grow up with a tragedy like that of my birth?! (*sadly*) Even my father . . . that poor fellow . . . they drove him too to his death . . . he carried death with him for others! (*energetically*) He never once agreed to this! But he was forced . . . he had no excuse . . . It's freedom . . . a life of dignity! (*distractedly*) He picked me up to kiss me . . . holding back his tears . . . I was then playing with other kids. He told me he'd be coming back soon! I asked about his travel . . . and these terrifying clothes . . . he looked frightening . . . (*with sad joy*) He told me he loved me a lot! (*regretfully*) As he got into the car . . . (*crying*) I ran behind him . . . I shouted at the top of my voice . . . father . . . father . . . and he waved as he disappeared further . . . and further from view . . . I was still running after him . . . running! I saw him wiping his tears away as he waved to me . . . until the car was lost to view! Until my father was lost to view! He hasn't returned yet . . . he's gone forever! (*weakly*) I never saw him again since that day . . . I was nine years old . . . just nine! What a waste! (*in despair and distraction*) Finally, I was alone . . . they all departed! My mother . . . my father . . . and that little goddess, my child . . . Lubna.

Even Lubna abandoned me to my sorrows . . . I've nothing left! Nothing! (*tired, he sits at the desk*) Nothing . . . the West Wind keeps blowing . . . the curse of the toilet . . . madmen . . . the putrid sands of the beach . . . and then the sea crab! Yes, the sea crab! That panicked crab and that terrified group of crabs! Not one crab remains on the sea floor!! They were crawling en masse to the beach . . . they dug their sharp and savage claws deep into the sand . . . biting and snapping . . . what horror! (*He falls silent, listening to the wind. He hums softly and distractedly, then repeats.*) Summer has passed . . . and no birds are left to sing . . . What should I do now that you have abandoned me? What should I do now that you have abandoned me? (*He hums, then falls silent listening to the sound of the wind.*) But, Lubna, why did you abandon me? I loved you . . . I worshipped you! How could you? How?! How could you destroy my life? I spent the best years of my life fighting for her . . . (*weakly*) I had no shelter . . . no food, and at night slept in railway stations, in stinking harbor warehouses with the rats! Daytime I spent under a hellish sun . . . and the suffocating fumes of chimneys! Just so I could obtain some living comfort! I had to do this alone . . . when I obtained it, you robbed it from me! You robbed me of everything!! (*standing, angrily*) And why? For the sake of that total madness which gripped you! (*in despair*) Those swaggering sorcerers . . . they robbed her of her mind . . . those conspiring thieves! That stupid head! The sharpest of daggers aimed at my heart . . . the heaviest rock chaining my manhood! How? How?! I cannot imagine. (*distracted*) My God . . . that little head! Who could have imagined!! When I first knew her . . . she was simple and naïve . . . kind and sweet . . . and that quiet sadness in her eyes that added to their charm . . . At one time she responded, from behind her sorrow . . . that she had no one in this world! She told me they were all buried beneath that rubble . . . in some mad night of war!! (*tenderly*) My heart almost burst with sorrow . . . I felt her close to me . . . very close! I felt I needed her badly to be by my side . . . since she shared something with me . . . the tragedy of my birth! The curse of my wanderings and my vagrancy! (*regretfully*) But she changed . . . changed utterly! She was no longer the person I needed! That naïve child!! That sadness which dwelt in her eyes . . . Everything changed!! (*uneasy and suspicious*) All of a sudden, she changed into a savage tigress! From the corners of her murderous jaws, blood dripped unceasingly . . . What misery . . . It was hard for me to believe! I left her that morning . . . only in the morning! When I returned at night, everything had changed! The eyes were not her eyes, and the hair was not her hair! Everything changed from when I had left her that morning! I looked for that green oasis in her eyes but couldn't find them! Her face . . . was a desert, its sands the color of burning sulfur! Even her hair . . . yes, her hair! That tigress needed to complete her appearance with that terrifying yellow mane . . . She was covering her head and face . . . yes, and even her eyes glowing with malice . . . were aflame!

(*in fear*) I didn't dare approach her . . . The horror! I almost lost my mind in the hell of these two eyes! I thought I had suddenly contracted some form of color blindness! But it was indeed she . . . that savage tigress! It was she lurking in a corner of the house . . . It was absolute madness! I didn't dare even to speak . . . to recover my Lubna . . . my friend . . . (*tenderly*) That beautiful roundness . . . that eternal embryo in the belly of the tigress was my child . . . which prevented me from voicing any objection! I wanted her to be happy . . . totally happy, and in every way! At my cost . . . at the cost of my own happiness! Yes, this is how I always treated her! We must all treat our pregnant women in this manner, for it is part of us that they carry and protect in their wombs! (*happily*) Can anything be more beautiful than that a person can see part of him grow and develop? Sucking on life in order to go out into it? And fill his world with happiness?! But . . . but . . . (*in despair*) How could she? How?! This has never happened in history . . . I know it well . . . Yes . . . it has never happened! Not one single tigress ever devoured its young! But that savage tigress . . . actually devoured her child . . . yes . . . murdered it! For Satan's sake, how could she? How?! That she would abort it with her own hands! With her two criminal hands! (*in anger*) That's a lie! A bare-faced lie! It was not a question of anemia! It was never a question of bad nutrition! Never! These physicians are all liars . . . All hypocrites! With her two criminal hands she did that deed . . . and at their suggestion! They helped her do it . . . and why? Because it was going to be my child! (*regretfully*) O God . . . I'd prepared the cradle! It never saw it! In the name of heaven, how do we allow the earth to receive our kids?! And before their cradles had received them?! Before they'd seen light on the path of life . . . though they are worthy of carrying its torch!? Its sacred torch. O God . . . that lovely face! Those eyes! (*weeping*) That little god?! How I comforted myself by thinking of it . . . to see that child playing with my things . . . with all things in the house! That it should fill my world with its charming cooing . . . to see it running happily on the beach . . . digging its tiny toes in the soft sand . . . and building its dream house with its child's hands. Meanwhile, I would join in its playing and joys, take it into my chest, and tell it stories, stories of Greek gods and beautiful princesses and sing to it the loveliest of songs . . . sweet songs of beauty and love, and forgetting, because of its magical smile, all the problems of life around me and all its hellish conditions . . . and that curse which cannot be effaced . . . Lubna! (*firmly*) We must do so! We must surrender every happiness in this world in return for the happiness bestowed on us by our children! We should offer them our souls!

(*pointing in pity to a female in the audience*) Have you seen his grave outside? There, by the entrance to the house! That tiny grave . . . (*smiling sadly*) It is pretty, is it not? (*regretfully*) All its flowers have withered . . . Lubna no longer waters them . . . and with her problems and madness she distracted me from it! A pity! But it's still pretty! (*weeping*) All these graves that hold our children . . . all are dear to us! (*repeats distractedly*) "Upon the never-ending beaches of the worlds, children are gathered, the tempest swirls in the air blindly, ships sink in oceans without a trace, death stalks its response, children play, upon the never-ending beaches of the worlds there is a vast crowd of children!" (*weeping*) Long were the hours I spent . . . in moonlight by its grave! I lost everything thereafter . . . all happiness! (*wearily*) And why? Because Lubna came to believe in freedom . . . the freedom of wolves is what they taught her! (*in anger*) What freedom? To destroy my freedom and build her own upon its ruins . . . to recover her stolen freedom in her wanderings and vagrancy . . . and recover the rights to life robbed from her by war from my freedom! Yes . . . to wrench out my lungs so she could breathe with them! They taught her this well . . . those wolves! (*rebelliously*) A curse on that freedom . . . and upon all who aspire to it! (*in despair*) Isn't this enough to make me lose my mind?! To make me run far away, even to hell! This is what they wanted me to do . . . (*firmly*) But I decided not to do so and to stand and face them all! In fact, I decided to take revenge, for myself and my freedom . . . to turn this hell that Lubna created for me into a hell for her . . . and for these wolves . . . and her insolent dog . . . the one she acquired to compensate for a child . . . and occupy my bed. I know well . . . Yes . . . that revenge is unlawful, whereas aggression is merely an infringement of the law . . . I'm a history teacher! But I decided to take revenge . . . and do so myself! (*nervously*) A law transgressed without deterrence is no law at all! (*in despair*) And for the first time! Yes, for the first time I would frequent a bar . . . yes, I, the teacher of literature and history! It was I who at night used to seek shelter in Lubna's nest! I started spending my nights with the riffraff, quaffing bad wine . . . that awful, deadly wine . . . hoping it would drive me far from Lubna . . . and her dog, and the hellish agony of being near her! I would return to her each night's end, totally drunk . . . I would throw at her everything that came to hand . . . In fact, I tore all her clothes to bits and threw them in the street . . . all her makeup . . . everything to do with her and her poverty! I wanted her to become housebound and die in her malice . . . (*triumphant*) She also did the same to me! But I no longer cared . . . those bastards fired me from my job and I'm no longer a teacher of literature and history! I'm no longer good enough to do so! Heh . . . and why?! Because I threaten their interests! Because I want their sons to live a life of dignity . . . ha . . . a threat . . . because I wanted to save their children from that madness . . . to make them avoid falling into the mud of their fathers . . . heh . . . What misery—a threat! (*He sits wearily at his desk, reaches out, and holds tightly the empty wine bottle. He contemplates it then tries to suck it dry, then puts it back in anger.*) There's nothing left . . . yes . . . these bastards fired me . . . destroyed my very last solace! But I shall not surrender to them! Never surrender . . . I can't surrender . . . so let me die of starvation, as they wish me to. They can paralyze and silence my stomach . . . as for my tongue, never! It's impossible that . . . (*suddenly silent, listening in panic to the sounds of a strong wind*) Once more, the West Wind! That mad and mighty wind . . . it is destroying my soul . . . it blows only to assassinate me . . . even the wind, damn it, they've enlisted on their side! (*in annoyance*) For hell's sake, won't that wind stop blowing? No doubt it hasn't left a single grain of sand on the beach! It must have carried them all away, exposing them once again! Oh . . . No . . . No . . . even if the god of winds himself . . . oh . . . my God! Impossible! I cannot imagine . . . (*listening to the sound of the wind, then jumps in panic and fear to the door*) The stomping of feet! At this late hour of the night?! How awful! Stomping . . . stomping . . . those monsters . . . it must be that they . . . they must have followed me to the beach! That bastard must have been hiding round the corner! (*retreating*) No . . . it can't be them . . . No one saw me when I went . . . (*listens again, then continues*) His heavy boot . . . that same boot . . . same stomping . . . he must be coming near my house . . . he's looking at the window . . . his gaze penetrates walls! No . . . it must be a horde of shoes . . . heavy, scary boots . . . the horde is creeping toward my house! (*the wind is heard clearly . . . shouting angrily*) Let these bastards stop their horrible marching! Let them silence the tramping of their boots! Silence these barbaric drumbeats . . . that ugly applause on the way to the gallows! (*He falls silent, the wind quietens. Then, in surprise*) They're moving away . . . away . . . (*in fear*) The same night . . . the same wind . . . the same madness! I was drunk when I came back home. I'd drunk all night, non-stop! (*in despair*) I found her weeping . . . She was hugging that damned dog of hers . . . I was tired . . . and needed her badly . . . I wanted to hug her . . . and cry on her warm chest! Each of us was on fire to torment the other, each of us was melting in the hell of that revenge blazing in our hearts. I had hoped we'd forget what was between us . . . the curse of revenge, Hera's curse, still flowing in our blood! I'd hoped we would begin our life anew . . . but . . . (*in anger*) She didn't give me the chance of that same madness! She drove me far away from her . . . she screamed at me like a mad woman . . . as though I were some wild beast! It's malice . . . that black malice eating her heart . . . that wild tigress! (*in rebellion*) At that point I lost my mind . . . I sprang at her . . . With all my strength, and desiring revenge, I grabbed the neck of that ugly dog . . . She resisted me . . . that spiteful tigress resisted . . . digging her paws into my neck . . . but I didn't let go . . . I took his life as he lay on her chest . . . and in her arms! (*wearily*) I never thought of killing her, not for a minute! I wanted her to be as pained and tormented as my love for her! But . . . that wretch! She fled outside like a mad woman, screaming at the top of her voice! He's gone mad . . . Sami has gone mad . . . He wants to murder me! Murder me! Murder me! (*in hysterics*) That wretch . . . I'm mad! The teacher of literature . . . and history . . . is mad! I ran after her . . . (*He stops suddenly, listening in fear to the wind and glancing at the door.*) The savage boots . . . Damn . . . they're approaching! They're coming near! (*rushes madly to window, draws curtain away, and looks outside*) That demon! It's the same one! The black cap! He's stopping . . . gazing at the window . . . his fiery eyes . . . he must have seen me when I buried her body deep! Fearing that crazy wind! (*retreating in fear*) That accursed wind . . . almost carried her away with the sand . . . the terror of it . . . the crabs in the sea left nothing of her! Those eyes! That beautiful mouth . . . Oh . . . How ugly . . . a horde of sea crabs?! She was a mere skeleton! A withered corpse . . . but how did this happen? How?! And so fast! (*in anger*) Where did that hateful wind come from?! (*returns to window, draws curtain away, looks out in anger*) He hasn't moved! His fiery eyes . . . (*opens the window in one burst*) What do you want, you wolf? Ha . . . you raging bull! You don't scare me . . . No, I don't fear your malicious looks . . . I didn't mean to kill her . . . You know this well! I never intended this . . . it was her nasty dog I wanted to kill! She did this to herself! She fled from her house . . . and ran like a madwoman to the beach . . . No doubt she wished to commit suicide! But I . . . I didn't . . . I simply wanted to lead her back . . . back from that madness! But she refused. (*hysterically*) Why don't you speak? Why not come to me? Why stand there like a statue? Heh . . . ? Why not say you saw me burying her deep in the sand . . . deep! You don't scare me . . . do you hear? You don't scare me! I've lost everything . . . She's over there, you wolf . . . on the beach . . . I strangled her with these two hands . . . over there . . . No . . . It was you who killed her . . . I did it at your bidding . . . I just wanted her back . . . she wanted to commit suicide! She dug her savage paws in my hand . . . I wanted to save her from that madness . . . She ran as fast as she could toward the sea . . . She almost plunged into the darkness of its terrible waves . . . (*springs madly to the door, then returns to window*) There . . . can you hear . . . You don't scare me . . . (*springs madly at the door and tries to open it*) I don't fear you . . . I will challenge you all . . . I will triumph over you . . . all of you . . . alone (*exits*) . . . Alone!

Glossary

Abaya: a simple or loose overcoat.

**Abu'l `Ala':** Abu'l `Ala' al-Ma`arri, poet and prose writer of immense originality, and of great importance in the history of Arabic literature, died AD 1058.

Astarte: the Greek form of the Semitic goddess named `Attart (Arabic `Ashtarut), goddess, among other things, of fertility.

Aures Mountains (of Algeria): the Algerian War of Independence commenced here in 1954.

***Children of the Alley*:** a famous novel by Najib Mahfuz.

Christophe Gbenye (1927–2015): Congolese politician and rebel.

Fida'i: Arabic for "self-sacrificer," a term often used for a member of the Palestinian resistance, usually an armed fighter.

Fatiha: the exordium or first chapter of the Qur'an.

Foreman Sayyid: a name meant to typify an Egyptian laborer working on building the High Dam.

Hera: wife of Zeus in Greek mythology, who placed a curse on Hercules.

Horus: Ancient Egyptian falcon god, one of whose eyes represented the sun, the other the moon, god of healing and protection.

Iram: in the Arabic tradition, an ancient city of great luxury destroyed by God for its sins. Mentioned in the Qur'an.

Jafr: a mystical book purportedly revealing the events of the future and attributed to the Prophet Muhammad and the Caliph 'Ali ibn Abi Talib.

Jahili period: the pre-Islamic era.

Jan Golian: Slovak army general of World War II who led an uprising against the Nazi occupation.

Kafr Qasim Massacre: a brutal massacre of farmers returning from their fields in this Palestinian village, carried out by the Israeli Border Guards on October 29, 1956. In total, forty-eight people were killed, of whom nineteen were men, six were women, and twenty-three were children aged eight to seventeen.

Khalid ibn al-Walid: celebrated conqueror of early Islam, died AD 642.

Khidr: in the Islamic tradition, a holy man who possesses great wisdom and mystic powers.

Liberation Army or Arab Liberation Army: an army of Arab volunteers, led by Fawzi al-Qawuqji, who fought in the 1948 war for Palestine.

Mutanabbi: one of the most renowned Arab poets of classical Islam, died AD 965.

Nakba: Arabic for "catastrophe," a term widely used to denote the events of 1948—the mass expulsion and displacement of around 750,000 Palestinians from their homeland at the time of the creation of the state of Israel.

Osiris: ancient Egyptian judge of the dead but also of resurrection and fertility.

Qumbaz: a traditional coat or jacket worn by Palestinian men.

Red wolves of Radfan: Yemeni tribesmen known for their militancy, who fought British troops during the so-called Aden Emergency of 1964.

Ridwan: in the Islamic tradition, heaven's gatekeeper.

Roderic: last king of Visigothic Spain, defeated in battle by the Arab Muslim army.

Sandala massacre: fifteen Palestinian students were killed, and several were injured, while returning home from school, by an Israeli explosive device hurled at them in the village of Sandala in 1957.

Takiyya: Islamic mystic convent or place of retreat.

Tariq ibn Ziyad: Muslim conqueror of Spain in AD 711.